George Wenninger

The Catholic Soldier's Guide

During his stay in India

George Wenninger

The Catholic Soldier's Guide
During his stay in India

ISBN/EAN: 9783337230043

Printed in Europe, USA, Canada, Australia, Japan

Cover: Foto ©ninafisch / pixelio.de

More available books at **www.hansebooks.com**

THE

CATHOLIC SOLDIER'S GUIDE

DURING HIS STAY IN INDIA.

BY

FATHER GEORGE WENNIGER. S.I

Bombay:
PRINTED AT THE "EXAMINER PRESS."—MEDOWS STREET, FORT.
1883.

PREFACE.

The object the author has in view in publishing this little book is to place in the hands of young soldiers, who have to serve in India, a friendly adviser, a good companion and guide.

By way of introduction, an old Soldier tells his story, how, in his time, men were enlisted and came out to this country. Things are now quite different, and greater advantages attend the young soldier under existing circumstances than in the time of the old East India Company.

Since the Troopships have begun to pass through the Suez Canal, the danger and tediousness of a voyage round the Cape has disappeared. On their arrival at Bombay, men are now better cared for, and, within a short space of time, they find themselves comfortably lodged in a military station.

What the author writes about the Bombay Presidency may be applied also to the other Presidencies. The first Chapters of the book are intended to lay the foundation for a good Christian life. The Chapter on Temperance and Temperance Societies is an important one for young and old soldiers alike. We next accompany the soldier through the various phases of his life in India : in hospital, in prison, and at school, and point out to him the many opportunities of self-improvement he possesses; the use he can make of his time and of his money. The married quarters, which are styled 'Patcheries' in India, are not so numerous now as they were ten years ago, before the introduction of the Short-Service system. However, mention had to be made of the married soldier's state, of his wife, and life in the Patcherie, and also of his children.

Old soldiers are getting scarce now. But it is a fact, that in many military stations they once formed the best and steadiest part of our congregations. After having led a dissolute life in their younger days, they turned over a new leaf, (at least a good many of them). Long and sad experience had taught them the right road. These were the men who attended at the evening devotions with great regularity; went to Holy Communion every month; were enrolled in the Confraternity; were generous in their subscriptions to Chapels and Schools; and kept away from the Canteen and from all those places, whence their misfortunes once originated. Almost all of them were natives of the Emerald Isle, most of them illiterate, but staunch Catholics, strong in their faith, who showed great respect for their clergy. And so were the Irishwomen, who still taught their daughters to courtesey to the Priest, as they had learned to do from their own parents in Ireland.

However, these remarks do not imply that young soldiers are all wanting in piety. On the contrary, we witness in these days many heroic actions of piety and penance done by young men in the ranks. As a rule, they have had the advantage of a better education, and have been brought up in one of those institutions which, through the exertions of the English and Irish Bishops, have been established in London, Liverpool, Manchester, Glasgow, and many other towns in England and Scotland, where Irish families are numerous. Some of them have enlisted, because they thought that such was their vocation ; some have run away from school and home to seek out the Recruiting Sergeant, by whom they have been relieved from present troubles. Such young men must be well cared for. By instruction, advice, and a little encouragement given to them with kindness and affection by a zealous Chaplain, they will become and remain good Catholics.

The young soldier is a stranger in this country, and perhaps during his whole stay he has no true friend to advise him. Thus, he is exposed to all kinds of dangers, surrounded by many occasions of sin; and when he once gets into bad company and used to bad habits, he cannot easily extricate himself. The Priest must be to him in the place of a parent ; and it can be proved by facts that the exertions of a sympathizing Priest have, in many cases, been crowned with great success.

It is but natural that such men, who spend only four or five years in India, should not look on this country as their home, and should constantly long for the day of their return to Europe; nevertheless a great deal of good can be done for them even during the short period of their stay. In the military service they have learnt habits of regularity, obedience to orders, and have had also opportunities afforded to them to improve their spiritual and temporal welfare. Many go back to Europe completely changed, and settle in life there under the most favourable circumstances.

Should this little book chance to fall into the hands of Catholic soldiers at Aldershot or Woolwich, who are under orders for India, the perusal of it will give them the most desirable information and warn them to be on their guard during their future career.

Each Chapter is illustrated by examples, all of which are real facts, many of them having been brought to the author's notice during the last fifteen years, during which he has been engaged in administering to the spiritual wants of soldiers in several Stations of the Bombay Presidency.

There are also several extracts from Butler's "Lives of the Saints," especially in Chapter V., certain critical notices which do not concern the ordinary soldier having been left out. Soldiers not unfrequently find such books as "Lives of the Saints" tedious; but they will take interest in short examples from the lives of holy men, who have distinguished themselves in the military profession.

CATHOLIC SOLDIERS,

Here then is a friend of yours. He wishes to be your guide and companion during your stay in India. You may have many other friends at home and abroad, but not every one you meet is a sincere, true friend. Many persons are your friends only as long as they can expect something from you, but in time of need, just when you are in want of their assistance, they forsake you. This is an every-day occurrence. It happened long ago to holy Job, as we read in the Bible. You may take it as a sure sign, then, that a man is your real friend when he perseveres and assists you in your troubles, in the hour of distress. False friends, deceitful companions, are often met with; such, I mean, as lead you to sin. A comrade who takes you to the Canteen, and causes you to become intoxicated; another who employs bad language; another who induces you to gamble; or one who shows you the most wicked places in the bazaar; all these are false friends who, under the cover of friendship, bring about the ruin of your soul and body, and thus injure your eternal and temporal welfare.

Now, listen! A true friend, a sincere companion, a valuable guide presents himself to you in the shape of this little book. Read the good advice and stick to it. There are different instructions here, which are calculated to enlighten you on certain very important subjects, and you will notice many hints concerning your religious and military duties. Take advantage of them! They are meant for you particularly!

Kirkee,   THE AUTHOR.
Feast of St. George, 1883.

INDEX.

CHAPTER I.
	PAGE.
§. 1.—The Military Profession	1
„ 2.—The Recruit	2
„ 3.—Starting for India	4
„ 4.—Arrival in Bombay, thirty-six years ago	5

CHAPTER II.
§. 1.—In a Military Station	7
„ 2.—The Library	8
„ 3.—On Joining the Confraternity	13
„ 4.—The Rosary	18
„ 5.—The Catholic Soldier's Evening Devotions.	20

CHAPTER III.
§. 1.—On Temperance	23
„ 2.—On Temperance Societies	36
„ 3.—Bombay R. C. Temperance Society	45

CHAPTER IV.
§. 1.—The Soldier's Salvation	50
„ 2.—The Soldier in mortal sin	57
„ 3.—The Soldier's Death and Particular Judgment	64
„ 4.—The Soldier fearing Hell	70
„ 5.—The Mercy of God	78

CHAPTER V.
Easter Duty	89

CHAPTER VI.
Calendar of Soldier Saints	102
St. Sebastian	105
The Forty Martyrs of Sebaste	106
Saint George Martyr	111
„ Pachomius Abbot	114
„ Julius, M.	119

S. S. Basilides, Quirinus or Cyrinus, Nabor & Nazarius, PAGE.
    Martyrs 120
Saint Jerom of Aemilian, C. 120
    " Victor of Marseilles, M. 122
    " Romanus, M. 126
    " Julian, M. 126
    " Adrian, M. 127
    " Ferreol, M. 128
    " Maurice and his Companions 130
    " Marcellus the Centurion, Martyr 134
    " Theodorus, surnamed Tyro M. 136
    " Martin, A. D. 397 139
§. 3.—A modern example of a saintly soldier. Joseph Louis
    Guerin 142

CHAPTER VII.

§. 1.—The Soldier in Hospital 148
" 2.—Care of the Body 150
" 3.—Care of the Soul 151
" 4.—How to spend Leisure-Hours 154
" 5.—The Chaplain's Visit 156
" 6.—The Last Rites of the Church 158
" 7.—An Incident of Indian Life 164

CHAPTER VIII.

§. 1.—The Soldier in trouble 175
" 2.—Behaviour whilst in Prison 179
" 3.—On being released from Prison 182

CHAPTER IX.

The Soldier's Self-Improvement... 184
§. 1.—The Workshops 185
" 2.—The Regimental School 190

CHAPTER X.

The use a Soldier can make of his money 198

CHAPTER XI.

	PAGE.
§. 1.—The Soldier who wants to get married	207
,, 2.— On Impurity	209
,, 3.—Choice of a Wife	221
,, 4.—On Mixed Marriages	227

CHAPTER XII.

§. 1.—The Soldier's Wife and Life in the Patcherie	234
,, 2.— Three days in the Patcherie after arrival from Europe	239

CHAPTER XIII.

The Soldier's Children	251

CHAPTER I.

§ 1.—The Military Profession.

The military profession is a very honourable one; this is proved by the fact that many heroes have belonged to it, and distinguished themselves as soldiers, in fighting for God, religion and country. Those who are called to this state of life should live in it as it behoves a true Christian soldier. For,

It is a Profession esteemed by Heaven.

Almighty God Himself, seems to be well pleased with it. In the Bible He calls Himself the "Lord of Hosts," that is, of Armies. The very Angels have served in His armies, when under the leadership of the blessed Michael the Archangel they fought against Lucifer, conquered him, and cast him into Hell. At least such is the image under which this event in God's creation is represented. In the course of time Angels frequently helped the Israelites, and Christian armies also, to conquer their enemies. Nay, St. Luke (II. 13), calls the Angels who appeared to the Shepherds during the first Christmas night, "a multitude of the heavenly host."

The Military Profession is also esteemed by the Catholic Church.

The Church, our mother, loves all her children alike, to whatever state of life they belong; but at the same time she esteems the military state in a particular manner, because she is much indebted to it for having defended and propagated the faith in many countries. Who is able to name all the soldiers, who have shed their blood for the Church, during the persecutions of the first centuries? Sebastian, Eustach, Mauritius, George, Porphyry, and many hundreds of other saints are patterns worthy of the imitation of all Christian soldiers.

The Military Profession is esteemed by the World.

It is the school of courage; it is the birth-place of heroes. The oldest and noblest families owe all their grandeur, in most cases, to this profession, in which their ancestors distinguished themselves. Even kings and princes have sprung from this state of life. If you have embraced it, show yourselves worthy of this dignity by good morals and a Christian behaviour in the barracks and field alike.

§ 2.—The Recruit.

Listen to what an old soldier says, who comes from Ireland, and has had long experience of the military profession, both at home and here in India. Between the spring and harvest time in Ireland there is always a dead lock both in town and country, amongst tradesmen, and labourers, and small farmers' sons especially, who are toiling from morning till evening on a small piece of land that will barely yield enough to pay the rent. These poor fellows go to some fair for a day's pleasure, and enter a dancing booth or tent to enjoy themselves. "I was among such people," says the old soldier, "when we met the Recruiting Sergeant with his party. He told us that soldiering was much easier than labouring. One of us took the Queen's shilling and, of course, his chum must take it too ; some fellows got the shilling slipped into their pockets and did not know a word about it till next morning, when they cried themselves sick at the thought of leaving a helpless family behind them. Indeed, most of the tradesmen and students, who give themselves up to the Recruiting Sergeant regret it afterwards, when they are ground down by the Barrack discipline, though they invariably make good soldiers. There are also a number of commercial travellers, and attorneys' clerks, discharged for drunkenness or dishonesty; ticket-of-leave men, also, who on similar occasions become soldiers, because they cannot do better. That evening we got some good punch from the Recruiting Sergeant, and for the first time in my life I drank two tumblers of it. Some fellows took three or four tumblers of it, and fell asleep. In the morning we were measured, and taken before the Medical Officer to pass. So the young gentleman, the farmer's son, the labourer, the clerk, and the ticket-of-leave man were all alike caught in one net.

"We were all draughted into the Regimental Depôt, soon attired in Her Majesty's uniform, and turned out to drill. The old soldiers gave us a hearty welcome, and knowing that we had received the bounty, they invited us to the canteen, and would not let us go until they saw our last farthing spent. After seven or eight months had elapsed, we had completed our course of drill, and drafts were prepared for India. The poor recruit was glad to get away from the Drill Instructor, and went on boardship ready to sail to any part of the world."

§ 3.—Starting for India.

"It was on the 15th August 1846, when we weighed anchor and started for Bombay. At that time the Troopships had to sail round the Cape, calling at Ceylon and Goa. We were over a thousand strong, counting men, women and children; but, strange to say, the old East India Company cared only for her soldiers' bodies, and no provision was made for their souls. The Church service was performed by the Captain himself, for there was neither Minister nor Priest on board. One Sunday, when we had just reached the Bay of Biscay, the service was suddenly interrupted by an approaching gale. "All hands on deck," sings out the Captain, and in a few minutes a terrible squall caught the ship on one side, so that the water rushed in in torrents. We were all employed pumping and shifting the ballast. Boxes were overturned, hurting many, and all night long, whilst this confusion lasted, we thought that we should perish altogether. Here you should have seen the old Irish women, with their husbands and children, praying to Almighty God to save them; but others, who seemed to have no religion at all, were blaspheming in the most fearful language. We Catholics wished for a Priest, but there was none, and so we could do nothing but pray and repeat our Act of Contrition over and over again.

"Thank God, the following morning the danger was over; the sun shone out, though the sea was still very wild. But there was another reason why we missed the spiritual consolation of a Priest. Erysipelas broke out, and not less than fifteen men died of it, and were consigned to the deep without the rites of the Church."

§ 4.—Arrival in Bombay, thirty-six years ago.

"On the 2nd January 1847 we arrived in Bombay Harbour. It was just after the cholera had swept over Kurrachee, and made such ravages in Sir Charles Napier's army. So we were kept in Bombay for ten days, and all taken to hospital. No Roman Catholic clergyman visited the sick; and, in fact, I thought there were no Priests at all in India. Yet we were in great need of a Priest, for many of our number died without Confession. Oh, happy days now, when the poor sinner has the opportunity of shaking off his load before he goes to his last place of reckoning!

Oh, Glory be to God, that the dying man can have the food of Angels administered to him before starting on his long journey!

As a rule, soldiers landing in India are in debt on account of different charges made against them on boardship, and also because they have to get many articles for their new kit. However, there was in the old East India Company's time a charge of a peculiar kind. It was called the COFFIN MONEY.

Indeed, the soldier on his arrival was at once put under stoppages to pay for his expected funeral. This arrangement was enough to frighten the new comer, and it filled his mind with serious reflections and anticipations. India is called the grave of British soldiers, because many die in the country, partly through their own fault, the diseases which they bring on themselves by their intemperate and licentious habits, and partly because the climate is injurious to them."

Such being the case, a man in India should take good care of his soul and his spiritual affairs. For, when in this respect all is correct he need not fear anything. I advise you, therefore, to read the following chapters with great attention.

CHAPTER II.

§ 1.—In a Military Station.

It will not be many days until the draft of each corps, or the whole Regiment arrives at the place of its destination—a military station in India. Almost everywhere the Cantonment is in the vicinity of a native town, and one or more Priests are in charge of the congregation, consisting of European and Native Christians. Now, when you are in your quarters, and settled, you must at once make inquiries where your Chapel is. Adjacent to the Chapel you are sure to find the Priest's house, perhaps, also a Convent or some other Educational establishment, which is conducted by members of a Religious Order or secular Catholic teachers. You are still a stranger in this country, and everything looks so different from what you have seen at home. But in the Chapel you will see a real home, and in the Priest you will discover a friend. After having given thanks to Almighty God for your safe voyage, you should make the acquaintance of the Military Chaplain, who will be very glad to welcome and advise you. He will tell you that there is also a Library near the Chapel, or at least some kind of accommodation for a Reading Room, where you can get a good book or paper to read. Some good Catholic men attend there, especially in the evening, and say together the Rosary in the Chapel. They chiefly belong to the Confraternity of Mount Carmel, and wear the Scapular. If there be no separate Temperance Society established, you will be at least in good company—among temperate men, or teetotallers, who do not make use of bad language and who pass their evenings in harmless amusements.

Your first days in camp are of the greatest importance, they may decide the whole future of a soldier in India. If you come to the Chapel and Reading Room, and say the Rosary every evening when you are off duty, and make it a rule to go to Confession and Communion once a month or so, you will have God's blessing and protection, and be free from many dangers and troubles. But, unfortunately, the majority of new-comers get into company of other kind. Perhaps, they meet a "towney", *i. e.*, one from the same town as themselves, or one who hails from the same county, or some other old soldier who introduces them to the Canteen, shows them the bazaar and such like places, which are the occasion of sin, and where they lay the foundation of a bad life.

In order to get at once a clear notion of the books and news-papers to be found in a Garrison Library, consider the following points, and afterwards make up your mind to read such books and papers only as may be of any benefit to you.

§ 2.—The Library.

There is no doubt but that a man who can and does read, will, by degrees, obtain higher and nobler notions, provided he reads suitable productions of the press. What a contrast is there between a soldier who passes his leisure hours in reading something useful, and the man who spends his time in idleness, in smoking, gambling and drinking! There are different kinds of useful books. Religious books must be mentioned in the first place, such as explanations of the Christian doctrine; Lives of the Saints; the History of the Old and New Testament, and of the Christian Church in general. The perusal of such books with attention cannot be too much recommended, especially to persons whose religious knowledge is deficient from want of a good education. By reading them you will get enlightened and strengthened in your faith, and will learn how to lead a good moral life.

In the next place, such books are recommended as afford secular instruction:—Historical works; Lives of heroes and conquerors; Descriptions of famous battles; of voyages and grand adventures. Likewise, popular editions of geography, astronomy, records and explanations of modern inventions and the like. English literature also abounds in many classical works belonging to every branch of prose and poetry, from the careful perusal of which you may learn a great deal, and refine your taste, improve your knowledge, and rectify your judgment.

Lastly, if you are not inclined to read books of a serious character, if you want only to amuse yourself and pass away the leisure hours in the Barrack-room,

you can also get good novels in every Catholic
Library, written by conscientious authors of the first
rank. You can see good news-papers, which have a
religious tendency, as, for instance, the *Bombay
Catholic Examiner*, the *Indo-European Correspondence*,
and others which are printed in this country. There
are also Home papers to be had, which give a correct
account of the religious and political transactions
all over the world.

But beware of false prophets! There are in certain
station Libraries, books, magazines, illustrated papers,
pamphlets, and tracts, provided for the use of soldiers,
which do great harm, fill your mind with doubts or
prejudices regarding your faith; and, though they have
on the clothing of sheep, they are inwardly ravening
wolves, as you will presently see.

In a Pastoral Letter the Catholic Bishop of Bombay
warned his flock against this danger. * He compares
the press of our time with the Tree of Knowledge of
Good and Evil. The fruits of that tree are books and
news-papers, good and bad. Our Holy Mother, the
Catholic Church, warns us incessantly with a loud
voice against bad writings. Thou shalt not read, for
otherwise thou shalt die the death. Bad are all those
books, pamphlets, periodicals, and newspapers that in
any way soever are directed against faith and morals,
against the Church and authority. And who can

---

* Leo Meurin, S. J., Titular Bishop of Ascalon, Vicar Apostolic
of Bombay and Administrator Apostolic of Poona, 15th February
1874.

deny that the amount of such writings has increased to a terrible extent? Thousands of novels, "fair to the eye and delightful to behold, "(Gen. II, 6) like the forbidden fruit of Paradise, are flooding the Book market. With very few exceptions these novels, written in a brilliant style, treat of illicit love and adultery, and offer to the excited imagination most indelicate, if not indecent and disgusting, representations calculated to vitiate a pure mind and to corrupt an undefiled heart. The destruction of pure morals brought about by such novels is only equalled by the extinction of the holy faith in those who indiscriminately read those newspapers, which the infidelity of our age has multiplied all over the world with such an astounding energy, talent, and sacrifice of gold, as have hardly ever been found in the service of truth and virtue. It is not possible to take up certain of these papers, without coming across a more or less frivolous attack on Religion."

The Pastoral winds up with an exhortation to establish Catholic Libraries everywhere, and to maintain Reading Rooms in the service of Religion as much as possible. It is a great pity that many soldiers by their subscriptions contribute to the maintenance of secular Libraries, and pay there for Protestant tracts and periodicals in which their Religion is ridiculed, nay, insulted. Perhaps they will answer that they want a variety of books and papers to read, which are not to be found in the Priest's

Library. But why are they not to be found there? Mainly, because so very few subscribe to the Catholic Library, not even enough to balance the expenses which the Priest has to incur for it even in the state in which it is. Let all the Catholic soldiers come forward and support a Library of their own; let them pay up regularly and generously their subscriptions and the Priest will be able to supply all their wants both in a religious and secular, but always Christian, point of view. Wherefore, the new comer to this country should consider it his duty to join at once the Catholic Library, and also to persuade others to do the same.

Next to joining the Catholic Library, the best thing a young soldier, after his arrival, can do, is to get enrolled in the Confraternity. In every military station, though under different names and rules, there is such a Confraternity for the soldiers. The one which is most widely spread is called the Confraternity of Our Blessed Lady of Mount Carmel, the members of which wear the Scapular. The whole organization and rules of this Confraternity are set forth in the "Garden of the Soul" (Edition for the army, page 291), which prayer-book is in every soldier's hands, so that there is no need of reprinting them here. But in order that you may properly appreciate this religious society, you must have clear notions concerning its advantages and obligations. Wherefore, read with attention this short chapter.

§ 3.—On joining the Confraternity.

Instruction on the Scapular.

In the year 1164, in the county of Kent, in England, the man was born who received the first Scapular from the Blessed Virgin herself. His name was Simon Stock. At the age of twelve he retired into a solitude, gave himself up entirely to prayer, ate nothing but wild herbs and roots; a little well supplied him with water to quench his thirst, and a hollow trunk of an old tree served him as shelter and bed. He had already spent thirty years in this manner when some monks of the Order of Mount Carmel, (Carmelites) came from Palestine to settle in England. Our holy hermit was informed of their arrival by the Blessed Virgin Mary, who appeared to him, saying, "Join this Religious Order, for it is very dear to me." Simon did not hesitate for a moment, and was happy to be received among their number. Then he made a pilgrimage to Palestine. Barefooted he visited the holy places, and at last reached Mount Carmel where he remained for six years. During that time he received extraordinary favours from heaven, and had a constant intercourse with the holy Angels, and especially with the Queen of all the Angels and Saints. One day she appeared to him, surrounded by a multitude of heavenly spirits, and handed to her servant the Scapular, saying, "Beloved son, receive the Scapular of thy Order, the sign of my Confraternity, a privilege for thee and for all the Carmelites. He who dies with the Scapular on, will not have to suffer the flames of Hell."

Now, what do you say to this promise? Could the Blessed Virgin have said anything better calculated to animate your confidence? The holy Fathers have written much about the rewards of pious servants of Mary, but none of them has, or could have, said so much. St. Bonaventure declares that Mary is all powerful in a certain sense. St. Peter Damian assures us that a soul, for which Mary prays, cannot perish. The abbot Guerier regards being under her protection as equal to being in heaven. Great promises indeed! But what are they in comparison to that which the Blessed Virgin made to Simon Stock? No wonder then, that, at the first rumour of this promise, Christians of all countries flocked to the Carmelite fathers to have their share of the treasure offered them by Mary. Lords, Princes, and Kings who have, no less than the poor, a soul to save or to lose, presented themselves to receive the Scapular. True, nobody can be absolutely certain regarding his eternal salvation, and whatever proofs we have of our being in a state of grace, still we must tremble when we think of the judgments of God, inscrutable and impenetrable as they are. We must work out our salvation, as the Apostle says, with fear and trembling. All this must be borne in mind to prevent our falling into error. When the Blessed Virgin promises us that by wearing the Scapular we shall escape Hell, the promise can be fulfilled on this condition only that we persevere to the end. Yet we are not without certain signs that we shall be saved. Devotion to Mary is one of these; and, in particular, this devotion of the Scapular.

About fifty years later the Blessed Virgin vouchsafed to appear a second time to Pope John XXII in order to recommend to him the Scapular. On that occasion she promised to assist in Purgatory the souls of those, who, during their lives on earth had been enrolled in the Confraternity and to console and liberate them on the first Saturday after their death. This is the second privilege which has been confirmed by many Popes in the course of time. However, in order to obtain these graces, certain conditions must be observed. As for the first promise, viz., that of a happy death, (1) you must have received the Scapular from a Priest who has power to give it; (2) you must wear it round your neck (and not in your pocket) day and night, and have it on you when you die.

As for the second promise, viz., *Delivery from Purgatory*—you must comply with the following conditions: If you can read, you must say the Little Office of the Blessed Virgin; if you cannot read, you must abstain from meat on all Wednesdays, Fridays, and Saturdays. But these conditions can be altered by any Priest, who has the power to do so.*

---

* Maurel; Indulgences, 1860.

The Scapular should be made of woollen cloth of either a brown colour or black. When you do not wear it, say for a whole day, you lose the indulgences for that time. Sometimes, soldiers, who fall into sin, think they are not worthy to wear the Scapular, take it off, and lay it aside. This is a mistake. Put it on again, for if you should be surprised by a sudden and unprovided death in a state of sin, you would go to Hell, although you had a Scapular laid by in your box.

As for the promise made by Mary, that those who wear the Scapular will be saved, we must not understand it in this sense: that a sinner by merely wearing it will go to Heaven. No, an impure soul cannot by any means be received into the society of the Saints. But we must be convinced that Mary obtains the grace of conversion which will prevent our dying in a state of sin. Mary makes use of natural means to change the heart,* and, by the grace of God, the greatest sinner may, if he does penance, become a Saint. But when a man resists the grace of God, and will not change his life; when he shuts his eyes to the light of salvation—then, he is lost. He dies in a state of impenitence, but he will not die with the Scapular on him. For, if Mary cannot prevail upon you to return to a state of grace, she will do one thing at least, and take the Scapular from you. Thus it happened to one who was going to commit suicide by drowning himself. He could not succeed. When he

---
* Colombière ; Sermon on the Scapular,

remembered that he wore a Scapular, he took it off at once, plunged again into the water, and disappeared. So he died in a state of sin by committing suicide, but he did not die with the Scapular round his neck.

But the Scapular affords also great protection to our temporal lives. At the siege of Montpelliér in France, the following happened in the sight of the whole French Army. A ball struck a soldier's breast, penetrated his uniform, but was arrested by the Scapular, and melted on coming into contact with it. King Louis XIII witnessed the miracle, and asked at once for a Scapular.

In 1866, when the Prussians were at war with the Austrians, another strange case occurred. At Aix-la-Chapelle 300 young men were summoned to proceed to the front. They were all good Catholics, and belonged to the Confraternity of Mount Carmel. Thousands of men were killed on the battle-fields in Bohemia; but these 300 remained uninjured, and when peace was concluded they all returned safe and sound to give thanks to God, who had protected them through the intercession of Our Lady of Mount Carmel.

Many books have been written on this subject, recording the miracles of the Scapular. You should read them in your Library, so as to strengthen your devotion, and also to induce others to get enrolled into this Confraternity.

Lastly, a great number of Indulgences are granted by the sovereign Pontiffs to those who wear the Scapular. Having complied with the usual duties of Confession, Communion, and Prayers according to the intention of the Pope, you may gain a Plenary Indulgence—

(1) On the day when you receive the Scapular;
(2) On the feast of Our Lady of Mount Carmel, which is the 16th July, or on any day of the Octave;
(3) On your death-bed.

Pope Clement X granted a Plenary Indulgence to be gained on the feasts of the Blessed Virgin, viz., on the Immaculate Conception; on that of the Nativity of the Blessed Virgin Mary; on the feasts of the Presentation, Annunciation, Visitation, Purification, and Assumption.

What a number of blessings may be thus received! What advantages! Go then, and become invested with the Scapular. It will be the best addition to your uniform, and be of more use to you than all the Victoria Crosses in the world. It is customary with the members of the Confraternity to assemble at the Chapel every evening when they are off-duty to recite the Rosary.

§ 4.—The Rosary.

This ancient, easy, and most familiar devotion is known to every Catholic from the days of his childhood. There are different prayers or meditations in different books; but that does not matter, and, in fact, every one can make his own meditations on the mysteries. The principal thing is to recite at each mystery one " Our Father" and ten " Hail Marys." Here in India we use the small Evening Prayer-book, which was first printed at Malta, and contains, besides the Soldiers' evening devotions, the fourteen Stations of the Cross, and the Office of the Blessed Virgin. No good Catholic soldier should be without it.*

But what must be particularly calculated to move you to say and attend the Rosary devotions is the great number of Indulgences the Church has granted to such as do so.

Pope Benedict XIII granted a Plenary indulgence to be gained once a year by all those who daily recite the Rosary. But for this purpose you must have your beads blessed by an authorised Priest. The blessing of the beads is of the greatest importance. As crucifixes, statues, or medals are blessed, in order that those who keep them may gain certain Indulgences, so it is also with the beads of the Rosary. But, remember, the beads which you have caused to be blessed, and which you have used in saying your Rosary, are only good for yourself, and when you give them to another person, they must be blessed anew, otherwise the Indulgences cannot be gained by the new owner. By using such beads Plenary Indulgences

---

* To be had at the Examiner Press, Bombay. Price 3 annas.

are each time gained, on the usual conditions of Confession and Communion, on the principal feasts of Our Lord and the Blessed Virgin; also on the feasts of the Apostles; on St. John's and St. Joseph's day; All Saints' day, and some other feasts.* The most privileged of all beads are those of St. Bridget, to which the greatest number of Indulgences is attached. One particular condition deserves to be mentioned, viz: you must hold in your hands the Rosary, during recitation; or at least the person who says the prayers in public with others must have a blessed Rosary in his hands. The Rosary contains the principal part of the soldier's evening devotions.

---

§ 5.—The Catholic Soldier's Evening Devotions.

A short explanation of the same may prove useful, and both enlighten and encourage many who hitherto have been strangers to them.

After having invoked the Holy Ghost, whose aid and grace are necessary for the right performance of all good works, we say—

The Angelus Domini.

It is an ancient pious usage to say this prayer, three times a day, at the sound of the bell, which is rung in the morning, at noon, and in the evening. By this

---

* Maurel—Indulgences of the Rosary.

prayer we honour and make as it were a profession of our faith in the mystery of Our Lord's Incarnation, which the Angel Gabriel announced to Mary. Every Catholic who recites the *Angelus* daily gains a Plenary Indulgence once a month. It is said kneeling, except on Sunday and Saturday evenings, and during Easter-tide, when the "*Regina Cœli*" (Rejoice, O Queen of Heaven!) is substituted.

After having finished the five mysteries, we add—

The Salve Regina (Hail, Holy Queen!) to which likewise many Indulgences are granted, and especially one at the hour of death can be gained by those who say it every day. Then follows the—

"*Litany of the Blessed Virgin*," commonly called the "Litany of Loretto." The titles under which we invoke her, such as "Mystical Rose," "Tower of David," "Morning Star," and so on, are taken from Holy Scripture and have special reference to Mary. Here, again, a Plenary Indulgence is granted to those who say it daily.

For the prayer of St. Bernard, commonly called the "*Memorare*" (Remember, O most Gracious Virgin Mary), Pope Pius IX, by a decree of 11th December 1846, has granted a Plenary Indulgence in a similar manner. The same applies to the prayer for "the Conversion of Sinners," and to that in honour of St. Francis Xavier for "the Propagation of the Faith," which are purposely said in order that you may gain the annexed Indulgences. For the Psalm, "De Profundis," you have an Indulgence of 100 days every time you recite it, as is done at the end of the Evening devotions.

So you see there is an accumulation of graces and Indulgences to be gained by practising these devotions. Happy the soldier who never fails to attend Chapel in the evening to assist at the Rosary and recite those prayers! He gains the blessing of God, the intercession of His Blessed Mother, the treasures of the Catholic Church. He obtains the most powerful help to lead a religious life according to his calling, strength to resist temptations, and consolation on his death-bed. Rest assured, the Blessed Virgin Mary will never forget those hours which you have spent at the foot of her altar. She will guide you through this stormy life; she will protect you in all dangers; she will plead your cause when you have reached the threshold of Eternity.

CHAPTER III.

§ I.—On Temperance.

By a "temperate man," is commonly meant one who does not exceed in drinking; and he who never tastes spirituous liquor is called a total abstainer. Temperance, however, as a Cardinal virtue, means something more than all this. According to St. Thomas, it is the moderation of every affection under the control of reason. In the Book of Wisdom (VIII. 7.) the word is called, Sobriety, and means the moderation of concupiscence or love of pleasures, especially those that consist in the sense of taste and touch. Since so many moral virtues are founded on temperance and depend upon it as on a hinge, it is a Cardinal virtue in the strictest sense of the word. The opposite vice of intemperance chiefly refers to excesses committed in eating and drinking. Hence, a man cannot be called temperate who avoids drunkenness only, but is a glutton in eating. This is a hint to certain members of Temperance Societies, who boast of being total abstainers from intoxicating liquor, but at the same time are not temperate in eating, nor moderate in drinking other beverages which are agreeable to the taste. How often do we not read in the papers about grand tea-parties in a Temperance Hall, on which occasions the members enjoyed their cakes and other good things without a thought of self-restraint? From this it follows, that a man may be temperate without being a total abstainer, if he never exceeds in eating and drinking, and a man may be intemperate, although he is a total abstainer, because he exceeds in eating.

In the whole creation it is man alone who can be intemperate. The reason is this:—Man consists of a reasonable soul and body. The Angels have no body, and therefore have no bodily wants. The animals have no reasonable soul and therefore have no spiritual wants. But man, because of his body, has sensual appetites, and these must be controlled by reason. When a brute eats or drinks, it is guided by natural instinct; and no horse nor dog will drink a drop of water more, when once it has had enough. Man has to be guided by reason, and if he be not so, he will be guilty and responsible for excess. Hence gluttony is one of the seven capital sins.

The danger of intemperance is the greatest when it is spirituous liquors that are indulged in without moderation. Excesses in eating may make a man sick; but alcohol flies to his head, and soon deprives him of the use of his spiritual faculties. Wherefore, what you read in the following pages on the advantages of temperance, and the baneful influence of intemperance refers to the use of spirituous liquors only.

Much has been said and written on this subject, so that it is almost impossible to say anything new upon it. But you will read facts and examples of daily occurrence here, which will surely astonish you and give a fresh colour to the whole affair, founded, as they are, on truth and reality. For some of them the author is indebted to a pamphlet written by an officer of the 95th Regiment, who was the President of a Temperance Society at Aden in 1863 and 1864.*

Temperance benefits the body and the soul. The advantages of a temperate life are therefore twofold— temporal and spiritual. Amongst the former, we must mention, above all, the good health of the body. It is true that certain teetotallers sometimes exaggerate the case, as though every alcoholic liquor was injurious to every one indiscriminately, and by publishing their eccentric opinions, they have more than once done harm to the cause of temperance. But there stands the fact, that the man who drinks nothing but water and such beverages as coffee and tea is generally in more robust health than the dram and pint and peg-drinker.

One of the ablest chemists of Europe, Professor Liebig (the inventor of the famous meat extract) states that, if a man were to consume eight or ten quarts of the best Bavarian beer every day, he would obtain in the course of twelve months no more nourishment than that contained in a five-pound loaf of bread.

---

* Five Addresses by Lieutenant Edward Chapple.

A London coal-heaver, a reformed drunkard, declared that from the time he took the pledge he could back sixty tons a day with perfect ease, whilst before that he could scarcely crawl home after such work, and was utterly unable to rise next day.

Dr. Jackson, a great authority on the health of armies, says that the use of ardent spirits is not necessary to enable a European to undergo the fatigue of marching in a climate, whose temperature is between 75° and 89°. He had had great experience himself in marching on foot, and had been employed in several operations in the field with troops in such a climate, and he never drank other beverages than water and coffee.

Livingstone, in all his travels and wanderings, through the red-hot sands of the deserts of Africa, in privations and fatigues of every kind, was always a water-drinker.

"I regard even the temperate use of wine," says Dr. Andrew Combe, "when not required by the constitution, as injurious, and it has been truly said that every healthy dram-drinker is a decoy duck, and no more proves that health is safe in intemperance, than an unwounded soldier proves that life is safe in battle."

In the Returns published some twenty years ago by the Government of India of the mortality of the troops it appears that amongst the abstainers eleven in one thousand died annually; amongst the temperate, twenty-five per thousand; and amongst the intemperate, forty-five per thousand. In the hospitals, the drunkards, and not the abstainers, are the first to be carried off by disease.

The men who contended in the Athenian games in the old days when Greece was in her glory, and whose bodily perfection was wondrous, drank nothing but water.

Many years ago some regiments were sent from Bengal to take part in the war in which the English were engaged in the Mysore country with the famous Tippoo Sahib. Several of the officers left Calcutta, labouring under incipient liver complaint; their faces were sallow, their cheeks sunken, their eyes glassy and hollow from that disease. During the contest many of them fell into the hands of Tippoo and were confined in a prison in Seringapatam. No wine nor spirits of any kind were allowed them; their beverage was water only. When the war was concluded, and the prisoners were released, they went forth from the prison walls with the bloom of health upon their cheeks, and no trace of disease was visible.

From these statements and facts it is clear that temperance, and particularly total abstinence is not injurious to the health and strength of the body. It does not *shorten* life, on the contrary, it *prolongs* it, as the ancient Anchorites prove. St. Paul reached 113 years of age, drinking only water, and having for daily food only a small loaf of bread.

But there is another advantage in temperance. It is conducive to the comforts of life; it greatly helps to make a man really happy; it secures to him a respectable position in the world; and the prospects of a soldier are particularly good when he abstains from drink. A sober man has fixed principles and acts upon them. He allows himself no extravagances, but only those recreations and refreshments, which tend to preserve life and good health. His kit is in good order; he has no debts. He never gets drunk. He keeps no bad company, and thus he is free from all the troubles which are the consequence of intemperance. There is no greater blessing on a family than a sober father, and a thrifty mother. Let them have small pay, and many children to provide for, yet they will do more with their little than others who have double their pay, but spend it in drink. You may see Non-Commissioned Officers' families who are always in want and misery, and many a private soldier, with a large family, is getting on well and contentedly.

Mr. MacGuire, a late member of Parliament, who wrote a very instructive book on "The Irish in America," states that all his countrymen there who are prosperous, owe all their wealth and respectability to their thriftiness and sobriety; but that drunkenness is the ruin of the most prosperous settlements. "A few years ago," he writes, "some hundreds of Irish families settled in Woolfe-Island. In the very commencement the profits of a good season were sacrificed to the fascinations of boon-companionship, and the indulgence of that passion so especially fatal to Irishmen. The evil was assuming alarming proportions, when the Priest resolved to grapple with it; and so powerfully and persuasively did he plead the cause of prudence and sobriety, so strenuously did he wrestle with the veteran drinkers, and such was his influence over the young, that he succeeded in enrolling eight hundred men in the ranks of temperance. The result was all that could be desired. Soon there was not a more prosperous or progressive settlement than that of Woolfe-Island, and now they are happy and contented, and are every year advancing in prosperity. Now see the

Spiritual Advantages of Temperance.

You need not be told how a temperate man edifies his neighbour and helps on the suppression of drunkenness by his example. For this reason many of the dignitaries of the Catholic Church have promoted the Temperance movement at home and in India, by pledging themselves to total abstinence and have persuaded many to become teetotallers. Many Priests have done the same, for the same purpose. Though, of course, in such cases, there was no necessity, on their own account for them to take the pledge. But the influence of good example counterbalances that of bad. Hence every temperate man, by his abstemious manner of life, encourages others to imitate him, and becomes in a certain sense of the word, an apostle of temperance, and may take to himself those words of the Prophet: "They that instruct many to justice shall shine as stars for all Eternity" (Daniel XII, 3). Nor is it necessary to dwell long upon the advantages of temperance so far as it is an act of self-denial, by which we can do penance for the sins of our past lives. For this purpose the Church recommends the law of fasting and abstinence. To abstain from alcoholic drink may be a great penance for persons who have at any time been addicted and used to it; perhaps greater penance than to abstain from meat, as the Church commands us to do on fast days. If, therefore, in a spirit of penance, they become teetotallers, it is a very real kind of satisfaction they give to Almighty God for the sins of their past lives. Many soldiers who are not obliged to fast, nor can do so, during Lent, abstain from porter and rum, and also from smoking, in order to keep to the spirit of the Church.

But there is another advantage of temperance. It inclines or helps a man to take care of his soul. The temperate man will also be a good Christian, and have religion in his heart. Members of Temperance Societies, if they are not given to other bad habits, will not find it difficult to make a good confession, or to approach the Table of the Lord, or in complying with all their religious duties. The sober man will pray, read good books, attend the Rosary and other devotions at Chapel, and find in them his true consolation.

Thus, he is esteemed by his superior officers; he gives no offence to his comrades; he is respected and loved by his Priest; in short, he is a credit to the whole congregation. If he has a poor mother at home, he will not fail to send her a few pounds every year, and the blessing of God is upon those who do not forget to support their parents in their old age. If a subscription for the Chapel, or the Orphanage be set on foot, he will be happy to give his share to it. If he is married, he will give a good example to his family, and parents and children will be united in peace and love, and the practice of religion.

Now look upon another portrait—the baneful influence intemperance has on body and soul. It ruins a man's temporal and spiritual welfare. These lines refer directly to the drunkard, not to the man who drinks with moderation. All the medical authorities are unanimous in the opinion that drink taken in excess destroys health.

The human frame in all its constituent parts is, so to say, made from the blood, bones, sinews, muscles, skin, hair, nails, *all* are formed from the blood. Whatever goes to make good blood tends to build up and strengthen the system; whatever does not make good blood aids nothing in forming the human body.

All our vitality is derived from the good blood in our system. But alcohol cannot assimilate with the human system, and never goes to make up any portion of the blood, on the contrary it reduces the digestive powers of the stomach; it nullifies the action of the gastric juice, reduces the volume of blood, and causes inflammation of that membrane which lines the stomach. The affinity it has for oxygen prevents the removal from the system of decayed materials, forms instead carbonic acid, and much decayed matter is retained, instead of being removed, and replaced by that which is full of life and health.

We have seen the advantages of temperance and total abstinence; they are beneficial both to soul and body, they make a man comfortable and happy in his social position, and in particular in the condition of a soldier. The disadvantages of intemperance are corresponding. Immoderate drinking destroys a man both in soul and body. Dreadful as the consequences are to a civilian, of indulgence in this vice, to a soldier they are more so. To him, more than to any one else, the virtue of temperance is indispensable. In his daily and hourly routine of life, subject to the unceasing supervision of those above him, it is incumbent on him to refrain from drawing upon himself the bitter fruit of addictedness to drink. It is with him an absolute necessity to keep from that vice, the practice of which entails so many, so severe, so prolonged punishments.

"Drunkenness is the invariable cause of *Courts Martial*," says the Duke of Wellington; and unhappily in our Indian army we must testify to the truth of this great Commander's statement. Now, think a moment on the long and painful punishment which drink entails on many of your comrades; you know the cheerless days and bitter nights they spend in narrow cells for faults committed through intemperance. The corrected prisoner sees, when it is too late, the fate to which he has doomed himself. From the Canteen his judgment has gone forth—it is there that he himself has framed the sentence. Lonely, he hears the bugle call to duty, but the sound falls sadly on his ears. For him there is no change. The heavy tread of the sentinel is the only sound through the long night to break the dismal monotony of his captivity.

In an address delivered on the 30th April 1864 by Lieutenant Chapple, the following example is related;—
"A few weeks ago, a man in the morning of life, with the red blood leaping in his veins, in all the strength and vigour of the prime of life, stood within a few moments of Eternity as the sun had just risen over one of the fairest spots in southern Europe: above his head was the scaffold, at his feet was the unconsecrated grave; around him stood his comrades with blanched cheeks, upon whose sinking hearts fell the sounds of the Dead March from the muffled drums. He was a Sergeant in the 2nd Bat-

talion of the 4th King's Own; four medals, won in hard fight, decorated his breast, and he stood there that morning, condemned to die a felon's death for having, in a moment of drunken rage, shot the wife whom he had sworn to protect. Nature was glad all round him; the air laden with the perfume of orange groves; the sunbeams were making silver pillars on the blue waters, and gilding the open grave, unconscious of the sad scene they were shining upon; all creation was singing its morning hymn of joy: but mingled with them was heard the solemn voice of the clergyman reading prayers for the wretched man, who stood within a few moments of God's judgment. He looked upon the glorious sight with the terrible consciousness that his own act was to shut his eyes with the seal of death, never more to open on earth, and that his own hand had dug the unconsecrated grave in a foreign land, far away from his home and friends. Before the fatal rope was adjusted round the swelling sinews of his manly throat, he asked permission to say a few words; it was granted to him.

"Comrades,' said he, 'see what a terrible fate I have brought myself to. It was drink brought me to this ending. Avoid drink; take warning by me," In a moment his career on earth was ended.

Drink is the source of all crimes; it fills the prison cells; it loads the convict ship; it throngs the workhouse; it crowds the lunatic asylum; it guides the steps, and nerves the red hand of the murderer; and it gives to the scaffold those haggard victims of despair. But bad and degrading as the vice of intemperance is to a single man, it is tenfold more ruinous to a man with a family. Let the father of a family drink but two drams a day; at the end of the year it amounts to eighteen gallons of spirits. See what clothes he could purchase for his children, with the price of those eighteen gallons! It is a terrible thing for children when their father is a drunkard. There are scenes in a drunkard's home that chill the life-blood in the heart; scenes from which human nature turns in horror, and weeps for the wretchedness of man; scenes at which the angels in heaven stand aghast, and wonder at the forbearance of God. Watch the children in a drunkard's home! From their gaunt and haggard cheeks, which the roses of health have never reddened, their unchild-like eyes, gleaming with unholy light, peer out with startling precocity on scenes of drunkenness; their young feet have early learnt the way to the Canteen to fetch the liquor for their parents, their young ears are familiar with curses; their thoughts are of the time when their father or mother will lie down in drunken slumber. No wonder, they will do as their parents have done.

Wherever you may turn your eyes,—to the broken healths, and broken fortunes,—to the broken hearts, and broken souls, you will discover the awful consequences of intemperance. You will see the hideous phantom of drink with its bloated face, its moist eye, and its swollen body and tottering legs, gloating over the ruin it has made.

Go to the hospital! There is one couch in that sick chamber at which humanity shudders and starts back, and religion turns away her head and weeps; one couch from which the loud, piercing shriek of madness breaks the silence of the night. *It is the drunkard's death-bed!* His eye is glassy and sunken; his tongue is swollen and black; his breath is fetid; his cheek-bones bare, and his cheeks, from which his own hands have torn the blossom of health, have fallen in. He is in the horrors of delirium. He is sinking rapidly. The doctor's art is now of no avail. Life is ebbing fast: he is within a few heart-throbs of Eternity. The conquered soul leaves the unworthly temple of the flesh, for the flesh has triumphed over her. The gates of death open, and the soul stands affrighted upon the shores of Eternity, and cowers beneath the glances of an angry God.

§ 2. On Temperance Societies.

The establishment of Temperance Societies has, especially during the last ten years, contributed much to lessen drunkenness in the army out here in India. There are different sorts of such societies.

1. *Regimental Temperance Societies*, which are usually patronized by a Commanding Officer, and with a view to exclude every religious principle, so as to induce Roman Catholics as well as Protestants to join them. In some places, however, where the Parson and certain religious ladies take an interest in them, these Temperance Societies assume a sectarian character. Protestant prayers are said, religious tracts served out, bigoted newspapers and periodicals distributed, so that a Roman Catholic soldier cannot, without sin and risk to his faith, belong to the Society. There is a great deal of attraction, even for Catholics, in a well-conducted Regimental Temperance Society. Not to speak of the refreshments provided in the Temperance Hall as well as in the Coffee-shop, they are amused by lectures, recitations, and songs occasionally; they have dances kept up nearly the whole night once a month—a privilege seldom granted by the Commanding Officer of a station to 'outsiders', who have to keep to their Barrack-rooms. Moreover, as the names of the members are known to the Colonel, they are the first on the roll for promotion, or for recommendation for some employment and the like.

The Soldiers' Total Abstinence Association was formed in Agra 1862. Mr. Gelson Gregson is the soul of that Society, and very cleverly managed to get it spread and approved of for the whole English Army, both in India and at home. The Annual Report for the year 1882 can boast of 3 Major-Generals who are Patrons, and Col. C. Ball-Acton, C. B., as President, and 68 Officers, Doctors and Protestant chaplains, who are Vice-Presidents. Mr. Gregson himself is the Secretary and Treasurer. When forming the branch Societies in 68 Stations, he always obtained first the sanction of the Commanding Officer, and by this means the Temperance Societies became "Regimental institutions," and gained the confidence of the men and the support of the Non-Commissioned Officers. A Commissioned Officer is appointed in many Regiments as the Superintendent, and inspects the accounts of the Society. The Report states that in India we have an army of 60,000 Europeans; of whom from 8,000 to 10,000 belong to the Regimental Temperance Society. No mention is made of a Catholic Temperance Association.

Mr. Gregson lays a great stress on the establishment of Temperance Halls, where the men can have their coffee and tea, without being obliged to endure the chaff of those who drop into the Regimental Coffee-shop fresh from the Canteen.

The Temperance Hall, he says, is to the abstainer very much what the Canteen is to the drinker. He found in one Regiment the Temperance Hall so well managed that it was more frequented than the Canteen. Wherefore he expresses a wish that these Rooms should be made as attractive as possible.

In order to get soldiers of all denominations to join the Regimental Temperance Society, Mr. Gregson laid down the rule, that religious discussions as well as political are not allowed in a Temperance Hall. The membership is also open to all ranks, women and children. There is one rule, however, against which Catholics must object, viz.: "That the second Monday in every month is observed by the members of Soldiers' Prayer Union and Bible Classes for special prayer on behalf of the Society."

One good suggestion is made, that all members on signing the pledge have their names taken off the Canteen roll, or have a mark placed against their names to prevent their liquor being drawn by others.

The services of Mr. Gregson in the Temperance cause were acknowledged by Government when, at the recommendation of the Commander-in-Chief, a free passage was granted him to Europe.

2. *The Good Templars' Society* was, several years ago, imported into India by Methodist preachers from America. The name of this Society is taken from that of the old Catholic religious Order called the "Knights Templars." This Order was instituted by seven gentlemen at Jerusalem in 1118 to defend the holy places and pilgrims from the insults of the Turks, and to keep the ways free for such as undertook the pilgrimage to the Holy Land. As their first house was situated near the

place where the Temple of Solomon stood, they were called Knights Templars. By the liberality of princes, immense riches flowed into this Order, by which the knights became (so it is said) puffed up to a degree of insolence which rendered them insupportable even to the Kings who had been their protectors; and King Philip of France resolved to compass their ruin. They were accused, (justly or falsely,) of treasons and conspiracies with the infidels, and of other enormous crimes, which occasioned the suppression of the Order, by a decree of Pope Clement V and the General Council of Vienne in 1312.*

Still some members continued to be united among themselves, in opposition of course to the rules of the Church. There is a secret tie between Templars and Freemasons, and they have almost the same signs, the same regulations, the same attitude towards the Church of Christ. One may assert, without exaggeration, that the Good Templar of these days is, though only outwardly and slightly connected with the craft, a Freemason who does not drink spirituous liquor. To say the least, if a Good Templar is not as yet a Freemason, he is on the road to become one. The Society of Good Templars is a secret Society, an imitation of, or a preparation for, Freemasonry. The attraction which this sort of Temperance people exercise, lies chiefly in their Masonic practices, and most men join them merely out of curiosity. It is

---

* Butler's Lives of the Saints, Vol. II., p. 572.

clear that a Catholic is bound in conscience to shun the Good Templars' Society, just as he is the Foresters and Odd Fellows.

3. *Catholic Temperance Societies*, based on religious principles, afford to the Catholic soldier in military stations the greatest advantages.

In Ireland, as everyone knows, it was the great and renowned Father Theobald Mathew, a native of the county of Tipperary, who first commenced the Temperance movement. He had been for some years one of the governors of the workhouse at Cork, where he daily witnessed the effects of strong drink among the poor wretched and broken-down waifs and strays of society. The dilapidated drunkard excited his compassion, but the orphan child of the drunkard made his heart bleed with sorrow. Some Protestant preachers had years before advocated the cause of Temperance, but, though they worked resolutely and bravely, they had not the ear and therefore found it impossible to reach the heart of the community, as Mr. MacGuire truly remarks in the Father's biography.* There was, besides, a lurking suspicion on the part of Catholics, who thought that these Protestant preachers only intended to entangle Catholics in their Societies.

After mature deliberation Father Mathew took the matter into his own hands. He convened a Temperance

---

* Compare Fr. Mathew's Life, by MacGuire, page 99.

meeting on the 10th of April 1838, and having declared in a short speech :—" I have come to the conviction that there is no necessity to take strong drinks for any one in good health—I advise you to follow my example:" he approached the table where the pledge book was laid, and said in a voice that is remembered by some to this day. "*Here goes, in the name of God!*" and signed his name. Every one knows how that small mustard seed became a mighty tree; how many hundreds of thousands in Europe and America were benefitted by taking the pledge of Total Abstinence. But God alone knows how many souls owe their eternal salvation to this great Temperance movement.

But there is one thing which particularly distinguishes Catholic Temperance Societies from all others. It is the *sacredness of the pledge*, (the banner of Religion), and the reliance on the grace of God. The latter is necessary to us for every act of virtue; without the grace of God we can do nothing profitable in the way of our salvation. Now, since the man who pledges himself to Total Abstinence is practising a great act of self-denial, it is clear that he must get from Almighty God the grace and strength to keep his promise. This divine assistance is obtained by prayer and the holy Sacraments. Hence, all the Catholic Temperance Societies make it a rule that their members should also comply with their religious duties. Let, therefore, a soldier who has taken the pledge attend the

Evening Devotions at the Chapel whenever he can; let him go, once a month or so, to confession and communion; let him pray for God's grace, especially during holy Mass, and he will have the most powerful help to persevere in his good resolutions.

It is not a Christian idea, much less is it a Catholic one, that a man is all right when he is a teetotaller only. Certain Methodist preachers extol Total Abstinence above every other virtue. It is true, on the one hand that intemperance is the cause of many other vices, but, on the other hand, we must not believe that a total abstainer is already a good Christian, if he does not practise other virtues; for it frequently happens that such a man is given to many vices,—especially impurity,—vices which he seems to have substituted for intemperance. A real good member of a Temperance Society is he only who leads also a religious life. This principle is a leading one in the management of such a Society. "Neither drunkards nor fornicators shall enter the kingdom of heaven." Wherefore, a man might die an unhappy death for other reasons than the vice of intemperance. In order to persevere to the end in a sober life, you must never omit your religious duties, and you must shun sin, whatever name it may bear.

In 1878 an old soldier was discharged from Her Majesty's 66th Regiment with five badges, a good conduct medal, and the bounty attached to it. This man had left home, whilst he was very young and foolish. The regiment was first stationed at Bangalore, and he carried on a very wild life in the line of drinking and other debauchery. One night, while returning from the Canteen quite drunk, he missed his way and fell into a ditch. There was about one foot of water in it, and as he was quite helpless, he remained lying in that ditch, fell asleep, and was picked up in the morning by coolies in a fearful state. His body was numbed by the cold water in every limb; his face was quite blue, and, in fact, people believed that he was dead. After careful treatment in hospital he came to himself again, and, on being told in what condition he had been, he said at once, "that was the last drop of the creature, I shall never taste it any more." So he went straight to the Priest, and took, at the steps of the altar, a most solemn pledge. At the same time he made a general confession, joined the Confraternity, attended at the Rosary every evening, received the Holy Sacraments once a month, and distinguished himself by extraordinary piety. He kept his pledge during the following 15 years, he stayed in Madras, Burmah, and various places in the Bombay Presidency.

It cannot be denied that as temperance induces a man to lead a good Christian life, so intemperance is the greatest obstacle to the practice of religion. A member of the Temperance Society gets to like to pray, to read good books, to receive the holy Sacraments, to shun fornication and adultery; whilst the drunkard can never make up his mind to lead a good life. Drink and nameless pleasures are always in his mind and in his way.

Of these Catholic Temperance Societies, we have now a great many in every Presidency. The missionaries in Madras have done their utmost to establish them in the principal military stations, and in those Temperance Halls the Catholic soldier can have all he desires. The Reverend Fathers Capuchins in Bengal, the Punjab, and the North-West Provinces work with great success in propagating the Temperance Society of St. Joseph. In the Bombay Presidency you have "under the protection of Mary Immaculate" a Temperance Society established by the Right Reverend L. Meurin, Bishop and Vicar-Apostolic of Bombay.

The following are the rules of this Society, and of them the 24th deserves particular attention :—

REVISED RULES
OF THE
BOMBAY R. C. TEMPERANCE SOCIETY,
Under the Protection of Mary Immaculate.

1. The Bombay R. C. Temperance Society is divided into several Branches, viz., for the civilians and for the several regiments and brigades of the army serving in India.

2. The Society enrolls as members only such persons as pledge themselves to total abstinence from spirituous liquors, either for lifetime or, in the case of soldiers, for the time of their stay in India, and then they form the First Class,—or for any other period, and then they form the Second Class; be they guided by the motive of preventing themselves from falling into the sin or vice of intemperance, or that of encouraging others to the practice of the virtue of abstinence, or that of offering to Almighty God an agreeable sacrifice, or by any other praiseworthy motive.

3. The use of spirituous liquors for medical purposes is considered to be against the pledge, except in a hospital or on a written order of the physician.

4. Persons, who desire to pledge themselves to the difficult task of partial abstinence, may address themselves privately to the Spiritual Director for guidance, and may, at his discretion, be admitted to attend the meetings, tea-parties and other amusements of the Society.

5. On entering the Society each member receives an Admission Card. The honours of the Society are the Diploma to be given to the members of both Classes after the first year of faithful observance of the abstinence pledge; a Silver Medal to be given to all after the second year, and the Veteran Bar to be given only to members of the First Class, after the third year.

6. Members of the Second Class do not receive the last honour; should they, however, enter the First Class, then their time of faithful observance of abstinence in the Second Class is to be taken into account.

7. The members pay a monthly subscription of 4 annas, whereby they are entitled to take part in the meetings and parties of the Society, and to receive the honours gratis.

8. No honours are given, unless the subscriptions are fully paid up.

9. Each branch chooses by a majority of votes its President and its Treasurer, for one year, in an annual meeting held for this purpose. Re-election is allowed.

10. The supreme government of the Society is in the hands of the Director, appointed by the Patron of the Society, the R. C. Bishop of Bombay.

11. In each Station the Chaplain is *ex-officio* the Director of the branches present in the Station. His duty is to admit or to dismiss members.

12. When taking or renewing the pledge, the member says in presence of the Director, on bended knees, before a crucifix or a statue of the Blessed Virgin Mary :—

" I promise to abstain from all spirituous liquor for my whole lifetime, (or, for the time of my stay in India) (or, for the period of......); and beg of Almighty

God, through the intercession of Mary Immaculate, to give me grace and strength to fulfill this my promise. In the name of the Father, and of the Son and of the Holy Ghost."

13. In each Station the members hold meetings, festivities, lectures, etc., according to their own wish or that of their Director and President.

14. A member who breaks his pledge, forfeits all rights and subscriptions already paid up, and is not allowed to use the honours in the meetings. On sincere repentance he may begin his first year again.

15. In the army, branches of the Bombay Temperance Society are formed according to regiments or companies and brigades or batteries, each of which has a President for conducting its whole business. In case of a regiment having detachments in different Stations, a temporary Vice-President is elected for each of the Stations, in which the President does not reside.

16. Each branch has likewise its Treasurer, and in case of division, its Vice-Treasurer. They deposit the money with the Chaplain.

17. At the time of the division of a regiment, the funds in hand of the Treasurer are divided according to the number of Members. On rejoining, the offices of the Vice-President and Vice-Treasurer cease, and the funds are amalgamated.

18. When different branches are stationed together, they join in common meetings and festivities under the guidance either of the Chaplain, or of a President chosen by common accord. Their funds remain separate, but they contribute to the common meetings according to the number of members.

19. The civil branches form themselves under their respective Parish Priests, who are their Directors *ex officio*.

20. They hold their meetings according to the discretion of the Director and the President.

21. The bearers of honours wear them in the meetings and in the Church on the feast-day of the Society.

22. The feast of the Immaculate Conception is the feast of the Society, on which all Catholic members are expected to receive holy Communion.

23. On the feast of the Immaculate Comception, on entering the Society, and on receiving an honour, each member gains an Indulgence of 40 days.

24. It is recommended to the members to join a religious Confraternity, to assist at the Evening Prayers and to receive every month holy Communion according to the pious usage of the Station.

CHAPTER IV.

§ 1.—The Soldier's Salvation.

God has made us to know Him, to love Him, to serve Him in this world, in order to be happy with Him in the next. We shall be happy with God in heaven, if during this life we work out our eternal salvation. That is our great and last end.

When you joined the army you did not think of that, but nevertheless the truth must be always before your eyes: "I have a soul to save or to lose." Perhaps you have heard or read something about the great St. Francis Xavier, the Apostle of India and Japan. He came out to this country in 1542, and converted many hundreds of thousands of heathens to the Christian religion. He was a saint; he worked countless and stupendous miracles.

But when he was young he was somewhat worldly-minded. One day St. Ignatius met him and said: "Francis, what does it profit a man, if he gain the whole world, but suffer the loss of his soul"? These words made a great impression on him, and he cared no more for the world, and only thought of his eternal salvation.

The same words I address to you, young soldier. You may have good prospects before you; but what is the use of all you can get in the world, if you lose your soul? Even, if in the next campaign, you should so distinguish yourself as to deserve to be decorated with the Victoria Cross; if you should obtain a commission in the army, and afterwards a respectable position in civil life: all this, if alone, is of no use, for you must also save your soul.

1. God made man according to His own image and likeness, and that likeness is in his soul. God is a spirit and so is your soul. God is existing in three persons; and so your soul has three faculties: understanding, free will and memory, the acts of which in a certain manner explain to us the mystery of the Blessed Trinity. God is immortal; and so is your soul immortal. Let the body after its separation from the soul become the prey of worms in the dark grave; let 100 and 1000 years pass away, and nothing remains of this earthly frame, but a handful of ashes; let the very monument that has been erected over the grave of a distinguished man have crumbled into dust; let the end of the world approach, the day of Judgment come and pass away: even, then, your soul will still live either eternally happy in the bosom of God, or eternally unhappy in hell. Hence, the Catechism says, that we must take greater care of the soul than of the body. The soul is indeed our noblest part, our own whole.

2. And when the soul of man became stained with the first sin, when man having thus obscured the image and likeness of God, surrendered it to the devil, its value only enormously increased on account of the

price, which Jesus Christ paid for its redemption. Ask then your Saviour what it has cost him to redeem your soul from the power of hell? Ask him why he came down from heaven? why he was born in a stable at Bethlehem? why he led that hidden life so many years at Nazareth? why he exposed himself to so many pains, to poverty, hardships and misery? why he suffered under Pontius Pilate, was crucified and buried? *For our salvation* he came from Heaven. Indeed, for no other reason did the Son of God become the Son of Man. Our salvation it was which drew from him a sweat of blood; this it was which bound him to the pillar, crowned him with thorns; for this he took the heavy cross upon his bruised shoulders, and gave his hands and feet to be pierced and underwent the torments of death. Ah, what do you think now of the value of your soul! God himself created that soul after his own image and likeness! The Son of God suffering, weeping, bleeding to redeem that soul; and man remains thoughtless, careless with regard to his immortal soul! But more than all this has been done for our salvation.

3. The work of our Saviour is still continued and will be so till the end of the world. Christ has established his Church, and left there the merits of his redemption: his word, his grace, the seven Sacraments, the Sacrifice of the Mass, his own Real Presence under the appearance of bread and wine. He commanded

his apostles to go forth into the whole world and to preach the Gospel. From the beginning the Church has sent out her missionaries across the ocean, and bid them live and die in foreign countries, sacrifice their health and strength, shed their very blood, if required, for the salvation of souls. You must not think that Priests and Nuns come out to India only in order to get a livelihood. No, the Catholic missionary, impelled by the love of God and zeal for the salvation of souls, and the Sister of Charity who has left her parents and relations, and renounced the pleasures of the world, have consecrated themselves to the service of God alone, to labour and suffer for saving souls.

But alas! How little do the greater part of mankind care for their eternal salvation! Whilst they do everything for the body, they neglect the soul altogether. The best years of life are spent in serving the body, but for the soul scarcely an hour can be spared on a Sunday morning.

The body is well fed; all means are procured to promote health and strength; but the poor soul starves for want of the nourishment she would find in hearing the word of God and receiving the Bread of Life.

The body is neatly dressed, but the soul remains in a filthy state, deprived of the garment of sanctifying grace, wallowing in the mire of vice.

To recover from bodily sickness, all means are tried, all doctors consulted, all medicines applied; but to recover from a disease of the soul from mortal sin. nothing is done. "O blindness of men," exclaims St. Augustine, "you deplore the death of a mortal body, and you are not troubled about the death of an immortal soul!"

Alas! What price, what value is set on that immortal soul by the Christian, who lives for months and years in a state of mortal sin; by the drunkard, who deprives his soul of sense and reason; by the youth who, to gratify his impure appetite, flings his soul, the image and likeness of God, into the mire; by the apostate who renounces the true religion and thereby tramples under foot the blood of Jesus Christ!

A priest who was giving a Mission in a village in France, passed one day a farmer's yard, where a groom was at the time busy in rubbing down his master's horse with great care.

My friend, said he, how many times a day do you see to your horse to keep him in good condition? I do not know exactly, replied the man, but I spend as much as two hours every day on the horse.

That is a great deal, said the Priest, and I see accordingly that your horse is very fine. But tell me, how much time do you give every day to the care of your soul to justify it, to sanctify it, to render it better, in a word, to prepare it for heaven? I will soon tell you that, father. Every morning I bless myself, I say an Our Father and Hail Mary. On Sunday I do not often miss Mass. That's all. Ah! my poor friend, said the Priest, since you take so little care of your soul and so much of your master's horse, I would rather be your horse than your soul. And yet what will it profit you, to earn a thousand francs a year, if you lose your soul? *

The care of your soul is, therefore, the most important business you have on earth. Every other business belongs to time; this belongs to eternity.

The question is not, whether you are to be rich or poor, sick or in good health, in disgrace or in honour, for a certain number of years. No, the question is, whether you are to be a citizen of heaven or an inhabitant of hell, a friend of God or an object of His indignation.

The question is about heaven and hell! I dare go so far as to say it is our only business on earth. For temporal losses may at least, in some measure, be repaired. If we lose one friend, we may find another. If we lose an eye or a hand, we have another still. But we have only one soul, and if that soul be lost the loss is absolute and eternally irretrievable. Your soul once lost is lost for ever.

---

* Noel, Catechisme de Rodez.

The salvation of your soul is your own personal business. Nobody else can attend to it, if you neglect it. It is true, God helps you with His grace. Your parents and friends advise you. Your Priests instruct you, but nobody can fight against your temptations. Nobody in the world can work out your salvation for you, if you yourself neglect your salvation: because nobody can perform good works for you. Your own virtues and good works, your own victories over the flesh, the world and the devil, and nothing else, will save your soul.

6. It must also be observed that your salvation is a very urgent affair. When you have to do a thing within a certain time, and when, moreover, that space of time is very short, then you must not delay; you must do it at once. Well, the time allotted to you for the salvation of your soul is very short and very uncertain. The thread of life may be cut at any period, and therefore you must begin that great important work at once. Delay is, Oh! how dangerous!

From all this you must conclude that the salvation of your soul is your greatest, or rather your only affair on earth.

Save your soul; for God has made it after his own image and likeness.

Save your soul; for Jesus Christ has redeemed it by shedding his blood for it. Save your soul; for the Holy Ghost has sanctified it, and Holy

Church supplies you with every means, and shows you the way to your salvation. No affair is more important, more necessary, more urgent, than the eternal salvation of your immortal soul.

§—2. The soldier in mortal sin.

About 1300 years ago there lived at Constantinople a very holy man by name St. John Chrysostom. He was a Bishop and also a most eloquent preacher; he was also a true follower of the Apostles, and without the least human respect he freely inveighed against the vices of his age. Theodosius, then emperor of Constantinople, oftentimes took offence at the strong language the Bishop made use of in his sermons, and on one occasion at a dinner-party he expressed his great indignation. His favourites proposed to him several modes of taking revenge. One said: transport him for life. Another thought it would be better to punish him by confiscating all his property; a third advice was for his immediate imprisonment, and a fourth one voted for his death. At last a general, who commanded great respect, rose up and said that not one of these punishments would afflict the holy Bishop. For, said he, if you banish him, he will lead the life of a holy hermit in the desert; if you confiscate his property, he will not feel the loss, because he spends all his money on the poor; if you send him to prison, he will embrace his chains, and like St.

Paul deem it a great happiness to suffer for the name of Jesus; and if you kill him, he will be venerated as a glorious martyr. So it will be no revenge nor punishment. But I give you this advice: get him to commit a mortal sin; for that holy man considers mortal sin the greatest evil in the world.

Indeed, there is no greater evil. The Saints of God were ready to suffer any loss, but they would not commit one sin for all the good and all the evil things in this world.

They knew and understood the malice of sin. The reason, then, why many men lead a sinful life is, because they do not reflect on, and therefore do not understand the evil of it. Now, what is sin? Sin is a wilful transgression of the law of God. By the law of God, I mean not only the Commandments of God and of His Church, but also the natural law, which God has written in every man's heart, telling him to do good and to avoid evil. The transgression is wilful when it is done with full knowledge and free will. You must know an order before you can disobey it. Not to hear Mass on a holiday of obligation is a transgression of a Commandment of the Church, and consequently a sin. But, when a man does not know it is such a day, his missing Mass on it is no sin, because of his want of knowledge.

Again, not to hear Mass on a Sunday is a mortal sin, but when duty prevents a soldier from hearing

Mass, it is no sin, because he is not free. There are however certain actions which are sinful though not wilful at the moment they are committed. So, when a man knows, that under the influence of drink he always makes use of filthy language, curses and blasphemes, he is responsible for these sins, because his drinking was wilful. He should not have got wilfully drunk, then he would not have committed the other crimes.

You always commit a mortal sin, when you wilfully break a Commandment in an important matter; you are guilty of venial sin, when the matter is not grievous, or when the action is wilful only to a certain extent To tell a lie is a sin. To tell a lie in joke or in excuse is only a venial sin; but if you tell a lie that injures your neighbour's character very much, you commit a mortal sin, because the matter is serious. But a good Christian should avoid even all sin, just because it is sin, and therefore displeases God. What you read in the following pages will give you an accurate idea of the evil there is in mortal sin.

1. Mortal sin is an offence against God. The grievousness of an offence depends on several circumstances as for example the high rank of the offended person, the low condition of the offender; the nature of the offence, the motives impelling a man to it, and also the persons in whose presence the offence is given.

Were your language or actions to insult the Commander-in-Chief, you would be more severely punished, than if you were to insult a Non-Commissioned Officer. Now in committing a mortal sin you offend One, who is infinitely greater than all the Kings of the world. It is He, who has made heaven and earth; the Governor and Ruler of the whole universe; the God of Abraham, Isaac and Jacob: the Supreme Being, all powerful, all wise, all just and most holy. Yes, He is insulted by you. And who are you? The creature of God, the work of his own hands, a worm of the earth, as the Scripture says. You rise like a rebel against God. You despise the laws He made for you, in order to make you happy in the world to come. But you say, at least implicitly: "I do not care for the reward which God has promised to the just in heaven. I am not frightened at the punishment which God threatens to inflict on me in hell. I will not serve Him; I shake off His yoke; I will have my own way."

O, the wickedness that is involved in every single mortal sin! And what induces a man to behave in this manner towards his Lord and good Master? If by committing a mortal sin you could get possession of all the wealth of the whole world, the enjoyment of all the pleasures of the world, the dominion over all the countries of the world: even, then, were you to commit a mortal sin, you would deserve to be called the meanest rebel against your King. But the reward of sin is not so great as this.

What induces men to offend God is a very trifle. For a few rupees, for a momentary pleasure, for a glass of liquor, many commit the greatest crimes.

Now, turn your eyes to heaven and see God on His throne surrounded by angels and saints that praise Him for His great power and glory whilst you thus insult the divine Majesty. Oh, who can measure the greatness of such an offence? I must say God alone can. For He alone can know and comprehend the distance between the Creator and the creature.

2. Mortal sin is also the blackest ingratitude against the best of fathers. All men, the very heathens, abhor him who is ungrateful, and who instead of thanks returns only insult and injuries to his benefactor. Now, God is our greatest benefactor; my existence, my redemption, the fact that I can obtain heaven I owe to Him, the faculties of soul and body He has given to me bespeak His bounty; that I awake in the morning in good health, that my heart does not cease to beat, that the blood runs through my veins and arteries, that I can see with my eyes, hear with my ears, speak with my tongue, work with my hands, walk on my feet: all this is a standing proof of the love and protection of God who constantly watches over me. And I know that were He to withdraw for a moment His arm from me, I should fall into nothingness. All grace again comes from Him—the Sacraments, the Sacrifice of the holy Mass, the countless and inestimable benefits He has left in the Church

remind me every day and hour of my benefactor. We read in the Gospel, that on many occasions our Saviour showed His mercy and love to sufferers by working miracles for their cure. Now, suppose that, having cured, say a leper, this man had turned against our Saviour and struck His face with that very hand that he had cleaned from leprosy: of what an ingratitude would not such a man have been guilty? Or, suppose that one of the deaf and dumb, to whom he had given the use of speech had repaired to Mount Calvary, and whilst the Saviour was in his agony on the Cross had begun to abuse and insult him with that same tongue that he had loosened! We shudder at the thought, our indignation is aroused, so monstrous would have been such ingratitude. But are we not doing something very similar when we commit sins with our eyes, ears, hands, with the faculties of the soul, which we have received from God's bounty?

3. More than this: sin is a desertion from the camp of Christ.

We were enrolled in the army of Christ on the day of our baptism. We were then sworn in to defend his colours, the holy Cross. But on the day on which we commit a mortal sin we actually go over to the devil, the enemy of Christ. Is he a loyal soldier who sides with the enemy? And if such a man were to be tried by martial law and sentenced, would the punishment inflicted by the Lord of Hosts on such traitors to Jesus Christ be too severe? The holy Fathers are quite right when they say that sinners betray and crucify our Saviour anew.

The greatest harm which you do by living in sin is done to yourselves. Take the case of a man, who after a good confession has received the Blessed Sacrament and turned over a new leaf, as the saying is; he will commit mortal sin no more; he is attentive to all his religious duties; he reads good books and keeps away from bad company. His soul is now robed in innocence; heaven is his own; by the tranquillity of a good conscience he already tastes in anticipation the joys of heaven. The angels rejoice, and are prepared to inscribe his name in the Book of Life. So he goes on for several days or weeks truly and happily. But the tempter draws near, takes him to the Canteen and other wicked places. He commits mortal sin. Ah, what a change has come over him! His soul is no longer an object of God's love. The dwelling place of the Holy Ghost has become the habitation of the devil. Peace is gone! The love of God is gone! Heaven is lost! The blood of Christ cries to heaven against that soul, because he has trampled on the blood that was shed for him; has made void the work of his redemption. The angels mourn over it. Hell opens to receive that soul, and the next moment may hurry it for ever into its abyss.

And, lastly, let the sinner think of the way sin is punished. How Adam and Eve by a single mortal sin brought such misery on themselves and on all their children. How the angels who followed Lucifer were condemned to hell; how so many who have sinned less, have had their lives cut short and are now suffering in hell. How our Saviour, to expiate the guilt of sin, suffered the most excruciating pains, and died on the cross. How so many penitents to satisfy for a single mortal sin have buried themselves in frightful solitudes and spent their lives in fasting and watching.

Oh, my God, what a monster a sinner must be! He offends Thee, who art his Creator and greatest Benefactor. He is an ungrateful wretch, this worm of the earth. He betrays the cause of Christ by deserting from his camp. He ruins his immortal soul. No more sin then! Oh, my God, who art infinitely good and always hatest sin, I beg pardon from my heart for all my offences against Thee; and I detest them all, because they are displeasing to Thy infinite goodness, and I firmly resolve never more to offend Thee and to avoid carefully all the occasions of sin.

§ 3.—The Soldier's Death and Particular Judgment.

It is appointed for men once to die, and after this the Judgment, (Hebr. 9, 27). In these words the Apostle speaks of that judgment which takes place immediately after death, and is called the Particular

Judgment, The great Universal Judgment on the last day is only a publication and confirmation of the sentence passed by God on the souls of men on the occasion of their Particular Judgment. It is this which makes death so terrible to every thinking and believing man. It is the awful account we have to give the moment we die.

Those who say they fear not death, because we all must die one day, little reflect on what follows death. We must not look upon death as though it were merely the end of our time on earth, but we must remember that it is the beginning of our eternity in the next world. This is a serious reflection. Cast your eyes on the very first step you must take beyond the grave! Consider, then, in this light the situation of a man the moment he expires with regard to Eternity! Represent to yourself a man in hospital in his last agony. He is stretched upon his bed, which he will not leave except to be taken to the dead-house. By degrees he loses his senses and the free use of his faculties, and you see him violently struggling with death, that draws near to sever the soul from the body, and to bring the soul into the presence of the Judge. The body will soon be a corpse. The eyes are broken and fixed, the feet and arms cold and stiff, the pulse is scarcely perceptible his breathing more and more hard and gasping, until the bystanders see he has breathed his last. Yes, even at that very moment his soul stands before the tribunal of God, which, according to the opinion of learned divines and pious writers, is in the very place where he has just died, beside the deathbed on which the corpse is seen lying. Now, give an account of thy stewardship! Thus said the Lord in the parable to the man, who had been accused of dishonesty in squandering the property entrusted to his administration. Who are you? A private soldier or a sergeant, or something more? How much have you in the bank? Are you decorated with a medal for having distinguished yourself as a valiant and gallant soldier? No such question will be asked. Your friends may speak about such things; your relations may be glad to get the money, and all the rest that belonged to you; a newspaper may mention your name and the distinction you have had in the world. But you will be asked other questions by your Judge.

What sins have you committed?

What good works have you performed?

What virtues have you practised?

What use have you made of the gifts and all the graces which God bestowed on you when in life?

The reply is already given in the Book of Life. Almighty God has seen and knows all particulars, and He will make them known to the whole world on the last day. How happy will be a soul that stands free from all stain of sin!

A soul that has not to fear either purgatory nor hell, such is the soul of a saint. But a few only are in such a case when they die. God is infinitely just and holy. Nothing defiled can enter heaven. Wherefore, the Church teaches that there is a place, called purgatory, where souls suffer for a time on account of their sins, that is to say, those souls which depart this life in venial sins, or which have not fully paid the debt of temporal punishment due to their sins, great or small. The soul, it is true, is in a state of grace, but not purified altogether, and now in the presence of the Judge the slightest stain of sin, however venial, is foul and horrible. Oh! what does not such a soul now feel for not having taken greater pain to please God and satisfy His justice during its temporal life! What grief will it feel for all its negligences in His holy service, in prayer and other good works; for those acts of impatience, lies, foolish idle words! Now, the soul perceives that it should have been more mortified, more charitable and humble, more fervent in gaining indulgences and making better use of the time it had on earth. But, alas! time is no more; divine justice can no longer be appeased by good works.

It is impossible to do any good, but it remains for the soul to suffer in purgatory for weeks, months, for years.

If such is the case with those who die in a state of grace, how terrible will be the situation of the impenitent sinner when standing before the tribunal of God! St. Paul wrote to the Hebrews (10, 31): "It is terrible to fall into the hands of the living God." This the sinner now experiences. He beholds an angry God and is struck with terror. He sees the world and cannot return to it. He sees hell and cannot escape it. Now, all the thoughts and words and deeds and omissions that make up a criminal life are spread before him.

Up to then he did not understand the wickedness there is in a single mortal sin. No; a weak memory, worldly principles and blindness of heart made him underrate the grievousness of an offence against God and made him incapable of at all comprehending it. But now his eyes are open; now he sees all his shameful sins, their number, circumstances and species. The whole judgment, the examination of conscience and the execution of the sentence is the work of a moment. The by-standers at that man's death-bed notice nothing but the fact that life is extinct. "What has become of him after death?" This question is already mentioned in the Book of Job. The dead body is there,—yes; but what has become of the soul? God knows that it has received its sentence.

From human knowledge all is concealed and remains a secret till the day of the Universal Judgment. The funeral is prepared. The *post mortem* examination of the body is over. The party warned for the occasion marches from the hospital to the cemetery, and in silent solemnity the coffin is carried to the grave. Here the Priest recites the burial service. He implores God to look down upon the deceased man with mercy, and sprinkles holy water on the coffin, that the dew of heaven, as it is called, may refresh his soul.

But *where* is the soul all this time? Has the man died in a state of sin? Did his Saviour meet him with a mild countenance, telling him, as the Priest prayed at his death-bed, that his place would be to-day in peace? Did the holy Angels and Saints receive him into their company, or did he die under the empire of Satan? All is a mystery. All we know is, that he had to give an account of his stewardship. The military honours are paid to his remains. The funeral party disperses, and the grave is closed.

What impression does the ceremony of the funeral make on the survivors? Alas, how few reflect on it! And yet we all must die, and then will all be judged. When? where? in what manner? God alone knows. Hence is derived every motive that loudly calls on us to prepare now for a good death. This preparation consists in leading a good life. Be then attentive to your religious duty; regular in receiving worthily the holy Sacraments; be sober, honest and chaste.

Men almost invariably die as they have lived. Those who lead the lives of sinners, ordinarily die the death of sinners, or at least is it not to be feared? And those who lead good and virtuous lives, commonly die the death of the just.

§ 4.—The Soldier fearing Hell.

Nothing is more certain than that Almighty God desires that all men should be saved. For this purpose he gives every man sufficient grace to work out his eternal salvation ; grace to keep his commandments, to resist and overcome all the assaults of the world, the flesh and the devil. And even, when a man goes astray, God does every thing, and so to say, takes every pains to bring him back.

At one time he calls the sinner by the voice of conscience, at another by sermons, good books, the advice of friends, or he sends him trials and troubles to bring him to his senses. But if after all these calls and warnings, the sinner remains obstinate, then the Almighty lifts up his arm, threatening him with eternal punishment in hell.

What is hell? A place where the sinner is deprived of the blessed sight of God ; is separated from God, his Angels and his Saints; it is a place of torments, fire, the worm of conscience to be endured for ever.

As the essential happiness of the Blessed in heaven consists in seeing God, knowing, loving and possessing him, so the essential torment of hell is the eternal separation from God. The moment God says: "Begone, ye accursed!" the damned are rejected by him for ever. *That* is damnation. Thus God is lost, heaven is lost, all is lost. Ah! what a terrible disappointment must it be, when a man, who has been rich in the world, in the enjoyment of all amusements and comforts, respected by all for his positon, abilities, achievements, as soon as he breathes his last, finds himself deprived of every thing—poor, miserable, rejected by God on account of his sins, excluded from heaven, and never more to have the least pleasure or relief from his sufferings.

There reigned once at Constantinople a Christian Emperor, called Zeno. But he had enemies who conspired against his life, and the Empress herself with them. One day when a dinner was given in the palace, the Emperor drank to excess and became insensible. His enemies gave out that the Emperor was dead. He was at once put into a coffin, and before he awoke from his intoxication was carried to the vault, where the Imperial family were buried. The heavy iron-gates of the vault were closed. Only after several days had passed, they were opened again, when it was found that the Emperor had been buried alive. Now imagine for a moment, the feelings of the Emperor Zeno, when he awoke from his state of intoxication and found himself in a coffin, locked up among the dead, soon to be like one of them!

But this conveys to our minds only a faint idea of the heart-break and the horror of a sinner on his first finding himself buried in hell. His sufferings begin at once. Let us endeavour first to get an idea of.

The Fire of Hell.

Even here on earth the pain of fire is one of the greatest we can imagine. To be burnt alive; to have burning torches brought near a person's body; to be laid on a red-hot iron grate or on live coals, to have the flesh torn by red-hot iron-pincers: such were the cruel tortures to which pagan tyrants condemned so many martyrs during the first centuries of raging persecution. Try only to hold your finger for one second in the flame of a candle, how painful it is! Perhaps you have some time or other seen one of those large furnaces they have in iron foundries—is it not a fearful heat, and an awful thing to go near and look at the crackling fire? Imagine that you were sentenced to be cast into such a furnace! True, you would soon be suffocated and dead. But if by a miracle God should keep you alive in that fire for a quarter of an hour, what would you not have to endure? And if you should remain in those flames for one hour—for a whole day—for a whole week—for a whole year? Oh God! we shudder at the mere thought, for it surpasses all we can imagine. And yet, that fire is only natural—an earthly fire. It destroys only the body, and after a short while it puts an end to our life. But the fire in hell is a quite different thing. It is created by God for the purpose of torturing the damned; it is a fire that acts on the very soul. The least degree of pain produced by the fire of hell is (according to St. Thomas) greater than all the excruciating pains the martyrs ever suffered. And, then, not to mention the other indescribable pains which through the senses torture the damned, no doubt, the worm of conscience is one of their chiefest torments. Our Saviour thus denominates the stings, the reproaches of conscience, the memory of past life and of crimes committed. Oh, how will not all the precious opportunities they have had and have misspent arise for ever against them! The fostering care of their parents; the advice they have received; the good examples they have seen; all the wondrous graces that have been lavished on them, but which they have despised and abused! Had they not heard of the joys of heaven and of the pains of hell? But they heeded *not*, nay, listened not, and now they are lost. The damned soul now clearly feels the self-reproach.

" I *might* have been saved, but I *would* not. Ah! if I had taken and followed the advice of my parents, of my friends, of my confessor! If I had only kept away from bad company! If I had never seen that young person again, with whom I became familiar and sinned! If I had been modest and had at once banished those bad thoughts, desires and imaginations, which were the cause of so many sins of impurity.

If I had always made good confessions, and had not from shame concealed such and such sins. Indeed, I might be now in heaven. And now I am among the *devils*, in that *fire* which will never be extinguished; in this *place* where the worm will never die; in this *prison* out of which there is no redemption. No, says St. Gregory, there needs no devils be in hell, no fire to make it a place of torments: the sins the damned brings with him into hell are tortures enough. But may one not say, that the most dreadful part of all this is that the fire of hell is never quenched, and that the worm will never die, in other words, the punishment in hell is eternal?

The Eternity of Hell.

All other sufferings must sooner or later end. This hope for an end is a great alleviation. How different is it with the damned! They suffer not only without a glimmer of hope, but they are in actual despair. Never will they obtain again one favour from God; never can they move His compassion; never appease His just wrath by all their sufferings. A soul condemned to hell a thousand years ago must exclaim: Hell is not for a thousand, a hundred thousand years, it is for ever!

Hear what the great orator Bourdaloue says on this subject: Can I represent to my mind this eternity? I figure to myself all the stars of heaven; to this innumerable multitude I add all the drops of water in the ocean; I reckon all the grains of sand on its shore. Then I ask myself: If I had for as many ages undergone torments in that fire, which is kindled by the wrath of God, would eternity be at an end? No! And why? Because it is eternity, and eternity has no end. To number the stars, to count the drops in the ocean, to tell the grains of sand that lie on its shore is not absolutely impossible; but to measure the number of days, years, ages of eternity, is what cannot be done, because its days, years, ages are without number, or to speak more properly, because in eternity there are neither days, nor years, nor ages, but a single, endless, infinite duration.

Oh Eternity that will never end! Serious reflection on this one word is enough to convert the greatest sinners. In 1769 there died at Lucca in Italy a saintly Archbishop,[*] Joseph Dominick Mansi. He had commenced life as a notary. One day, being obliged to go to a house, where he had probably some will to make, he passed a church where a sermon was being preached. Impelled by curiosity, he entered and soon perceived that the preacher had taken for his subject the eternity of hell. From time to time he passed and electrified his audience by crying out: "Oh eternity that will never end." The tone in which he pronounced these words, produced an extraordinary effect on Mansi. He left the church, absorbed

---

[*] Schmidt et Bellet, Cat. Hist. II, 569.

in thought, and went on his way; only now and then he stopped and repeated to himself: "Oh eternity that will never end!" Returning to his house, just as he was about to sit down to table, an interior voice seemed to repeat the same words in his ear: Oh eternity, that will never end! By night as well as by day, alike at prayer and at business, that important sentence sounded in his ear and occupied his mind. Touched, at length, by this celestial warning, he left the world, became a priest and later on a real exemplary Bishop.

Let every man have a proper fear of eternal punishment, such a one will never sin. Think of hell, and you will escape it, as St. Augustine says. See who are in hell, what road leads to it, and ask yourself, whether you are in danger of going there. Who are in hell? Men, who on earth made little of religion, transgressed God's Commandments and those of the Church. Are you one of them? If you are of that number behold your place is in hell! Who are in hell? Men who took the name of God in vain, profaned the holy name of God by cursing and swearing. Are you one of them? If you are, behold your place in hell! Who are in hell? Bad parents, those who gave scandals, the unchaste, the drunkards, the impenitent, those who neglected their Easter duty, apostates, those who belonged to secret societies forbidden by the Church. Have you committed and are you still committing mortal sin? Behold your place in hell!

Away, then with, mortal sin! Keep from it and repent. One Act of perfect Contrition, made even at the last moment of life, extinguishes the fire of hell. Always make good confessions, and you will have a passport which will give you admittance into the kingdom of heaven.

CHAPTER IV.

§ 5.—The Mercy of God.

It is dreadful whilst in a state of sin to fall into the hands of the living God at the moment we die. It is consoling and encouraging to know that God is infinitely merciful and long-suffering as long as we are in this world. God is infinite in all His perfections, and, therefore, none of them, none more than the other can be called greater or smaller, and yet, in regard to mankind, God's power, wisdom, providence, immensity and eternity seem all to have a share in manifesting His infinite mercy to us. "Thy mercy is magnified even to the heavens," (Ps. LVI. 11). Therefore, the mercies of the Lord I will sing for ever." (Ps. LXXXVIII. 2).

It was surely out of His goodness that He created the universe, and assigned to our first parents such a beautiful dwelling place as the Garden of Eden. Still much more was his infinite mercy manifested, when, they having committed sin, He at once, there and then promised them a Redeemer to atone for, and give satisfaction for their sin. The whole history of the chosen people of God is one long series of merciful dealings of patience and long-suffering. But how were these all surpassed in the fulfilment of time when the second person of the Blessed Trinity took our human nature, to live, to suffer, and to die in it for us. Mercy and love were the prominent features of the character of Jesus, God made Man. In one of the eight Beatitudes, he pronounced in his sermon on the Mount, he declares : " Blessed are the merciful for they shall obtain mercy." By word and example he, all his life-time, encouraged poor sinners to trust in the mercy of God. When we read in the Gospel of those frequent conversations with sinners, we must observe that he had for his sole object to reclaim them from their wicked ways, and bring them to the ways of justice and eternal salvation. On one of these occasions (he was eating in the house of a publican, as St. Luke relates in the 15th Chapter of his Gospel), the Pharisees were greatly scandalized; but our Saviour in reply told them that it was the great end of his mission on earth to seek sinners and convert them, that is, to win them to His mercy; those in good health need not the physician, but the sick only; so he had come not for the just, but for sinners. He has left us two parables, marvellous pictures, both of them, of the mercy of God towards sinners. These, are "The Lost Sheep" and "The Prodigal Son." In the first parable a shepherd, who has one hundred sheep, misses one. Leaving its companions in safety, he goes after the lost sheep ; he seeks it till he finds it, then he lays it upon his shoulders, and carries it home with joy. Here we have a graphic picture of himself and of his conduct. He is the Divine Shepherd who follows the sinner, pursues him, moves him by his grace, and at length brings him back to the flock in this way. How often have the greatest sinners been thus converted to God? Count, if you can, the hermits of old who have left the world and retired into deserts, there in solitude and silence, by works of penance, prayer, and watching, to atone for their past offences! It was the voice of the Good Shepherd that called and brought them from their once sinful life to their holy one. Penetrate with your eyes the interior of monasteries and convents, and how many similiar witnesses to God's mercy will you find there! How many soldiers, wild and dissolute in their youth, whilst they indulged in drink, who committed fornication, and were in the habit of cursing and swearing, were at last found by the Good Shepherd, obeyed His voice, and corresponding with grace, turning over a new leaf, and keeping their good resolutions, are now happy and content and as it were already at home; how many good Christians and true soldiers of Christ are to be found, bearing witness in their sufferings to the mercy of God.

The other parable I referred to as that which our Saviour related on this occasion is the parable of "The Prodigal Son." A greater enemy Religion never had than Voltaire, who lived about 100 years ago, and even he used to say that he never read this parable without shedding tears.

A young man, one of two sons, and the younger of them, who had obtained from his father a portion of the family fortune, to which he had certainly no claim during his father's life, left his parental home, and went to some distant country, where he led for a while a very bad life, and spent all his money in debauchery. He soon fell into the depths of misery,— as soon as his money was spent, he lost the friends he had made; then a famine visited the country, and he was glad to take even the lowest service,—to attend to the swine—and he was fain to satisfy his hunger on the husks given to these animals.

Seeing himself in such misery, he began to think of his former condition whilst in his father's house, and made up his mind to return. So he went halfnaked, filthy,—a true representation of a man in the state of sin. What will his father say? How receive him? Ah! a long way off his father saw, and knew him. Full of pity, he did not wait until the poor boy had prostrated himself at his feet, but he ran to meet him, embraced and kissed him, had the fatted calf killed and made a great feast—for " this my son was dead, and is alive again; he was lost, and he is found again." We know what the feelings of a tender father are, and how the greatest offences are forgiven when a child submits and asks pardon. But there are certain sins which cannot be pardoned at once, nor without reproaches, to make the offender sensible of what he has done. And surely the case of the Prodigal Son was such a one. But Almighty God in His mercy acts in a different manner. Jesus Christ being the Friend of repentant sinners receives them at once wtihout uttering a single word of reproach, and he himself related this parable in order to show us the kind of reception every poor sinner will meet with, if only he has made up his mind to do penance. Ah! this soul was dead and is come to life again. Jesus embraces the repenting sinner, covers him with the garment of sanctifying grace, arranges a great feast, and at the great entertainment gives him His own flesh and blood in Holy Communion. Then all the angels are invited to rejoice with the Heavenly Father over the conversion of that sinner. " For this my son was lost, and he is found again." Thus did Our Lord receive Mary Magdalen when prostrate at his feet, she wept for her sins! The Pharisees were scandalised. "Many sins are forgiven her, for she has loved much," were his words.

Jesus Christ is indeed the Friend of repenting sinners. See, how he deals with Zaccheus. This man (who was the chief of the publicans) sought to see and to become acquainted with Jesus. When Jesus came near his city, he climbed into a tree that he might see Him. But Jesus looking up called to him: " Zaccheus, make haste, come down, this day I must abide in thy house." The people murmured at his intention to be the guest of a man who was a sinner But Zaccheus standing afar off, said: "Behold, the half of my goods I give to the poor, and if I have wronged any man, I restore him fourfold." Jesus replied: "This day is salvation come to this house, because he also is a son of Abraham. For the Son of Man is come to seek and to save that which was lost." Listen to all this, all you poor sinners. Come to Our Lord Jesus, trust in his mercy! On the day of your conversion he will abide in your house,—in Holy Communion, he will be your guest, and truly you may say: "To-day salvation is come to this house."

Not less touching is the reply Jesus made to the Pharisees when they had brought to him a woman taken in adultery. According to the law of Moses, such women were to be stoned outside the city. But Jesus said (John VIII. 7.): "He that is without sin among you, let him cast the first stone at her." And they went out one by one, leaving the woman alone. Then Jesus asked her: "Where are they that accused thee? Has no one condemned thee?" She said "No man, Lord." And Jesus said: "Neither will I condemn thee,—go, and sin no more." Yes, go in peace, thy sins are forgiven thee! Blessed words of absolution! and *his* words, for in his name we dare to utter them. How often have they been repeated by the Priests of God during the last 1800 years! Go, and sin no more.

Let us now turn to the closing scene of Our Saviour's life, and there see what his mercy is! Death is the echo of life. What a man has said and done during life, he repeats at the hour of death. Now, since mercy and love for repentant sinners so distinguished Jesus Christ through life on all occasions, we shall surely find them shining in all splendour at his death. The hour of his death has come. His hands and feet are nailed to the Cross, and His divine head is crowned with thorns; the blood trickles down from innumerable open wounds to the earth. Seven times he spoke, and what he said is known as the "Seven last words of Christ on the Cross." And which was his first word? "Father," he exclaimed, "forgive them, for they know not what they do." He calls on God: "Father," the sweetest name a son can pronounce. "Show not Thyself as the Almighty, nor as the severe Judge, but as a Father. Here I am hanging on the Cross; I have been obedient even to the death of the Cross; I have done everything Thou hast commanded me, but now listen to my last dying request. Father, forgive them for they know not what they do. Forgive Pontius Pilate, forgive the High Priests, forgive the false witnesses! Forgive the cruelty of my executioners, forgive the ingratitude of the people who cried, 'Away with him, let him be crucified,' forgive these Scribes and Pharisees who at this moment insult and blaspheme me; they know not what they do." Surely they could not be excused on the ground of ignorance; but Our Saviour would show his mercy and love towards them.

What sinner then will despair when he meditates on the mercy of God! If Jesus Christ prayed for those who nailed him on the Cross, will He not be ready to forgive all the sins you have committed? God Himself tells you: "I will not the death of the sinner, but that he may be converted and live."

To continue the work of his infinite mercy he instituted the Sacrament of Penance. He gave the power of forgiving sins to his apostles, and to their successors, to the end of the world, and this all for the sake of penitent sinners. Is not the Confessional a standing monument of the mercy of God? Were a king to empower all the judges throughout his dominions to forgive all sorts of crimes to any one who should apply for forgiveness, how merciful and good would he be! And, behold, such is the power which Christ has given to his Priests: "Whose sins you shall forgive they are forgiven," and observe, the Priest in Confession is not only a judge, he is also a father to console, help, and encourage the sinner; he is also the physician who heals the wounds inflicted by sin; he is surely the truest of friends to the sinner who complies with the conditions required for obtaining pardon. Let a man have been as bad and as infamous as possible, hated as his crimes deserve, there is always one who will not show or feel aught but true love for him, or have aught but the kindest words for him, and this one is he who represents Jesus Christ. He loves his penitent, and treats him as Jesus Christ has done.

Without allowing one moment for repentance were God at once to punish the sinner, (as he did the fallen angels); were he to send fire from heaven to consume the rebellious sinner, were the earth to open under his feet and swallow him, at the moment that he transgresses God's holy law; indeed, that sinner would have no reason to complain. But the Lord would still be just, and his judgment just. But, O mercy of God! He does not punish us at once, nor the second time, nor the third. How long do we try his patience. How often, and how dreadfully do we provoke him, and still he is ready to embrace the sinner at the first sign of penance.

And what kind of penance is required? In former times the Church imposed severe penances. For example[*] one who had consulted a fortune-teller had to do penance for five years; one who had done servile work on Sunday had to fast for three days upon bread and water. A child who had cursed his parents had to fast forty days. Persons who had committed sins of impurity had to do penance for three, ten, or fifteen years, according to the nature of the offence. Now, the discipline of the Church is not so severe,— and this should be another reason for the poor sinner to have recourse to the mercy of God in the Sacrament of Penance.

We read in a book of respectable authority, the following almost incredible story. I tell it to you, as

---

[*] S. Carol. Barom. Instruct.

though I were showing you a picture in order to bring vividly before you the inconceivable goodness of God to him who is sincerely penitent. There lived in Milan a certain wicked wretch who, though learned, hated God, and committed all sorts of crimes, not from ignorance of their guilt, nor overcome by temptation, but with the wilful intention to offend God, whom he so much hated. Hearing of a catalogue of sins drawn up by a certain professor of divinity, he got the book to read it and see if there was anything new in the way of sin to him; and there was one sin, and only one he had not as yet committed, namely, Sacrilege. So he forthwith went to a saintly old Priest for the express purpose of making a sacrilegious confession. He began to enumerate all the horrible crimes he could think of. The Priest listened attentively without a word of reproach. "But, Father," said he, "do you not hear what I have done? I have committed all these sins out of pure malice." "God is good and merciful." said the Priest, "he will forgive you." "But supposing I came only to make a mockery of you, and of God, how then could I obtain pardon?" "Even then," replied the Priest "provided you were only to repent. God would forgive you."

Hearing this the wretched sinner melted into tears of extreme sorrow for his sins. So great was his emotion, and so vehement, that a blood vessel burst, and he expired in the Confessional, before the Priest could give him absolution. The latter was of course very much troubled at the event. But the next day, as he was saying a mass for his soul, he heard a mysterious voice; " God sends me, I am saved. Thank you for the kindness and love with which you received me yesterday. Oh, it is true, God is infinitely merciful!"

CHAPTER V.

Easter Duty.

It is strange, but, alas! it is at the same time true, that the majority of soldiers out here in India do not comply with their Easter duty, I mean do not go to Confession and Communion at Easter or thereabouts, according to the two Commandments of the Church:

1. To go to Confession at least once a year (4th Com.)
2. To receive the Blessed Sacrament at least once a year, and that at Easter or thereabouts. (5th Com.)

Since Jesus Christ has instituted the Sacrament of Penance for the forgiveness of sins, and Holy Communion in order that we might have "life eternal," it has been from the beginning an established law to go to Confession and Communion. When and how often the faithful should communicate was not determined by Christ Himself. In fact, the fervour of the first Christians rendered such an order superfluous. But when, in course of time, piety grew cold, so cold that Christians used to pass years without going to Confession and Communion, the Church, in the General Lateran Council (1215) made the law, that all should do so once a year under pain of excommunication. To neglect, then, this Easter duty is a very grievous sin, for the Church does not inflict such a great punishment as excommunication for a transgression that is not very grievous. Now, supposing you have neglected your Confession and Communion at the last Easter season, can you wait till the next season comes round? No, the earliest opportunity, as soon as possible, you are bound to comply with your duty. As one who has failed to pay his debts within the time appointed is obliged to pay them as soon as ever he can afterwards, so he who has not complied with his religious duties at Easter, must do so as soon as possible.

This Confession you can make to any Priest authorized to hear Confessions, and in any place you like. But when it is practicable you ought to receive Holy Communion in your own Parish church.

Again, though the Church thus obliges us to confess and communicate once a year we should not be satisfied with this, but we should oftener go to Confession and Communion. A good Christian soldier or civilian will receive Holy Communion on all the great feasts during the year, and if he be a member of the Confraternity, on every first Sunday of the month, according to the Rules.

The Reverend F. Darien, a Missionary among the wild tribes of North America, relates that he once met with Christians in a deserted place, who for three whole years had been without a resident Priest. Now attend to what follows. Every year they had gone the 300 miles that lay between them and the next parish in order to get Confession and Communion. 300 miles! and along what kind of road had they to travel! Oh, shame on those who have a Chapel and a Priest in their station, and yet neglect their Easter duty for years and years.! And what judgment have they to expect after neglecting so many graces?

But what are the reasons and causes, why so many soldiers keep away from Confession and Communion? Many causes might be assigned. The following three will perhaps account for most of this deplorable neglect:—(1) ignorance; (2) human respect, indifference and sloth; and (3) the love of one's sins or evil ways.

1.—*Some neglect their Easter duty out of ignorance.*

A man who is ignorant as regards religion, cannot know the duties of his religion nor the importance of these duties. Unfortunately there are many in the army whose education has been neglected. They did not go to a school long enough to learn to read or write; they have had no parents nor any friend to look after them. In order to earn a little money, they have been compelled to work in a factory or in a farm-yard, and so years passed away until they took the shilling which has fixed them where they are. In this manner young soldiers come out to India, men who have never made their first Confession and Communion, as ignorant of their religious duties as on the day they left home as children. They have heard nothing about religion, but only know that they are Roman Catholics. On Sundays they are marched to Chapel, and, of course, understand very little about the service. They hear the Priest speaking from the altar or the pulpit about Confession and Communion, but they do not know what it means. If they had anybody to teach them how to make a good Confession and Communion they would gladly learn. Now they feel shy and ashamed of their ignorance, and so they remain for years in the same ignorance and in the same neglect. How often do Priests in India meet with such cases in the hospital! How many a soldier makes his first and last Communion on his death-bed! Now such should put away their shyness and shame and ask their Priest for instruction in their religious duties. If they can read, (only a slight knowledge of reading will be sufficient to read the Catechism with fruit) they should get a Catechism; if they cannot read, they should not despair nor delay from year to year their Easter duty, but with great courage and confidence in God learn, as they easily may, what is necessary for their eternal salvation. The author of this book would say to the uninstructed soldier: " Fear not to go to your Priest; he will be happy to instruct you!" In fact, without *private* instruction such men will never be sufficiently instructed. Then let them pay great attention to the sermons on Sunday, and to all the instructions that are given in the Chapel, and soon they will assuredly know how to prepare for a good Confession and a worthy Communion.

2. *Many neglect their "Easter duty" out of pure weakness, that is to say, out of human respect, indifference and sloth.*

They would like to receive Holy Communion, but they are afraid of Confession. It is true that to make a good Confession may be hard, especially when one has neglected it for a long time, or has committed certain sins which he would not like to mention to any one. It may require courage to show the hideousness and ulcers of the soul; it is a great humiliation and a thing quite against nature to kneel before another man and tell the secrets of one's heart. But, nevertheless, there is no help for it, Confession is the only remedy. Confession will not be so difficult as you imagine when you consider that at any rate it is better to tell one's sins to the Priest, who is bound to secrecy by a most solemn law than to live in a state of sin and die an unhappy death. Remember that the Priest is there only to absolve and not to condemn you; to heal your wounds and not to irritate them; to console and encourage you and not to humble you; to excite your sorrow and shame, but only with a view to wash your sins away. The Priest will keep the secret of the Confessional, even at the loss of his own life. He is a sinful man himself, and he every day prays like you; "Forgive us our trespasses." You may be sure that you cannot tell him anything new. You may be equally sure that he will have compassion on you, and that he rejoices in reconciling you to God,—all the more rejoices, the more you have offended God. On the Day of Judgment all the sins we have not confessed will be laid bare before the whole world. It is not, therefore, so difficult to make a humble Confession to the Priest, and you ought to prefer it to that confusion which you will have to suffer on the Day of Judgment before all the Angels and before all men. But it is God himself who will make it easy for you. Then, again, very many soldiers neglect their Easter duty simply out of carelessness, indifference, and sloth. They perhaps regularly say their prayers every day, come to Mass, and, though not marched, nevertheless go to Benediction on a Sunday evening; they are good, honest, sober, exact in the performance of every other duty, but with regard to Confession and Communion they are quite careless and indifferent. It is not want of faith, but thoughtlessness; they do not take the trouble to fulfil this chief duty commanded by the Church. Such men should remember that the kingdom of heaven must be gained by violence, and it is not the slothful, easy-going Christians who are worthy of it. 'Not every one who says, "Lord, Lord!!" will enter into the kingdom of heaven, but he who does the will of my Father who is in heaven.'

The Church commands us all to make our Confession and Communion once a year. Thus by neglecting Confession and not going to Communion, you disobey the Church, and therefore you disobey God. Regarding this disobedience, Christ has said: "He who does not hear the Church, let him be to you as a heathen or a publican." But it is clear, that neither unbelievers nor public sinners who die in a state of impenitence will be saved; therefore, this one simple neglect of your Easter duty (if you die with the sin of it on your conscience.) prevents your eternal salvation. You may be good and honest in every other respect, but if you do not go to Confession and Communion as the Church commands you, all the rest of your religion is in vain. Remember what St. James says in his letter (Ch. II. v. 10. 11.): "Now whosoever shall keep the whole law, but offend in one point is become guilty of all. For he that said, 'Thou shalt not commit adultery,' said also, 'Thou shalt not kill,' Now if thou do not commit adultery, but shalt kill, thou art become a transgressor of the law."

3. *Finally, Wickedness of Life is the great cause of many omitting their Easter Duty.*

They assuredly may be termed wicked who do not wish to give up their bad habits. "What is the use of my going to Confession," soldiers often say, "if I do not change my life"? Indeed, their refusing to abandon their sins is a very sad thing to think of.

Nor will they leave the occasions of sin, that is to say, the persons with whom they have committed it; the places in which they have been in the habit of offending God. They hope to return to God some day, and make peace with him—at least they wish to die in a state of grace; but, not *now* while they are in India, they say, not whilst they are in the army; not whilst in the midst of so many temptations to sin. Thus they delay their conversion. Delay is the great stratagem of our enemy. True God has often granted the grace of conversion to many sinners on their death-beds. The good thief on the Cross is such an instance. Those who come at the eleventh hour will receive the same reward as those who came early in the day. Many a soldier who has obstinately refused to go to Confession has at the last moment had the Priest at his bedside and received absolution. But these are the exceptions, not the rule. How often does it happen, that the Priest is called too late, or not called at all, or that no Priest is to be had?

To delay one's conversion and at the same time hope for God's pardon before death is marvellously like the sin of presumption, one of the sins against the Holy Ghost, of which Christ says, that they will not be forgiven, either in this world or in the next. Does God promise or grant the grace of a happy death to every one? Quite the contrary. Hear the awful threat which our Saviour uttered against the Jews: " You shall seek me, and you shall not find me, and you shall die in your sins."

And this is in accordance with what the prophet Isaias says: 'Seek the Lord whilst you can find Him; invoke Him whilst he is near you; for the time will come when you cannot find him, and He will not hear your prayers.'

"Not that you should suppose that there are any circumstances, under which mercy is impossible at the hour of death; as long as life lasts, the greatest sinner may still obtain pardon of God, and one act of contrition and pure love of God is enough. Let no one then despair of his salvation; let every one hope to hear those words which our Blessed Saviour spoke to the penitent thief: "This day thou shalt be with me in Paradise." But the fact is that old sinners, who for years have gone on neglecting the grace of God, for years refused to go to Confession, for years delayed with their eyes open, are usually surprised at last by a sudden and unprovided death.

Such was the case with an Artillery man at Colaba in 1874. He was like many another who turned a deaf ear to the Priest's advice. He did not even feel sick, but on a sudden God called him to his account. A blood-vessel broke, caused his death, and he had not even time to say, "Lord have mercy on me." How many an old drunkard has been suffocated in his sleep, and found dead in the morning without having been able to make one act of contrition!

Some years ago a time-expired man went home.

He was repeatedly advised by the Priest to make his Confession before he embarked, but he would not, and did not do so. He died on boardship without the assistance of a Priest, and was buried in the Red-Sea.

In 1869 a battery of Artillery marched from Kirkee to Mhow. The Priest exhorted the men to go to Confession and Communion before starting, and there was some reason for it, because on the line of march a number of men always died of malarious fever as they passed through the jungles. On one occasion no fewer than twenty men died in those jungles, and since then the road is known to officers and men as the "Dead March." Well, the Battery was only one day's march from Kirkee, when a man died of cholera. He was a Catholic, and unfortunately one of those who had neglected their Easter duty.

Sickly men sent to a sanitarium for a change of air should always avail themselves of the first opportunity of going to Confession and Communion, when the visiting Priest arrives at the place. For it often happens that men take a sudden change and there is no time to send to the next military station for a Priest, and so they die in their sins.

We call it a death-bed conversion, when a man living in sin obtains from God the *external* grace to have a Priest at his side to hear his Confession, and the interior grace to make it. But these conversions are not always sincere ; they are always doubtful, because they are caused merely by the prospect of death. But for this the dying man would have gone on deferring his conversion. Were this fear removed, he would go on deferring it for a still longer time, and probably return afterwards to his former ways as many others have done. Were he sure his illness would not end in death, he would neither confess nor think of doing so. As long as there was no danger, he thought little of his sins and less still of doing penance for them. Wherefore, his grief seems to have been caused by *nothing* that God can accept as a just motive. Is it not evident that he never meant to embrace God's service until the world and all the opportunities of sinning were slipping out of his hands? Does the motive which prompted him differ from natural fear, the view of the grave, the near prospect of eternal punishment? Take away that fear, and where will be his repentance ? Gone!

It is not a thing of rare occurrence for soldiers who have received *all* the rites of the Church. Absolution, Communion, Extreme Unction, the Last Blessing, when at last they have recovered from their illlness, to return to barracks and lead the same bad life as before. And can we call such conversions sincere ? And if not, could such conversions have gained heaven for them? This opinion is rather severe, for the sinner may be well disposed when receiving the last Sacraments, but afterwards his will changes, as is often the case with penitents in good health. However, we can only judge from facts; it is God who searches the hearts.

But there is another side of the question. Putting off conversion in this way, no doubt, increases the difficulty of a good Confession. Now that you are in good health and can quietly go to Chapel on an evening to prepare for a good Confession, all is very easy and can be done properly. But when you have not been to your Easter duty for years, and sickness comes upon you, fearful pains perhaps in the body, and great troubles of soul, when you are in a hospital ward, among a number of Protestants, and the Priest is sent for only a day, or as it may happen, half an hour before you die, how difficult is it then to prepare for and to make a good Confession! Think what a good Confession means, involves, implies! It implies the making an examination of conscience, the recollection of all the sins of so many years, the confession of them, the number of times you have been guilty of them, and the circumstances which have aggravated them. Now, though you are in good health, you say that you are not prepared to make a good Confession; you want time for it, and thus you evade the invitation of the Priest again, and again, and again. It is difficult to pray and prepare for Confession when we suffer only from a headache or the like. But how difficult must it be when we are on our death-bed, seized with the pangs of our last agony? Then perhaps a man may make a sort of Confession, but without any preparation. The Priest has only time to ask a few questions. Where is the good act of Contrition so much required for a good Confession? Where is the penance you should perform for the sins of your past life? What difficulties attend a death-bed repentance on every side? Therefore go to Confession in proper time; do not delay your Easter duty; receive the Blessed Sacrament, often during the year and you will be prepared for a happy death.

CHAPTER VI.

Many soldiers, young and old, often say: "As long as I am in the service, I cannot lead a religious life." No better argument against this prejudice can be brought forward than the fact, that such a great number of soldiers have not only distinguished themselves by their piety, but have become great Saints, as the following Calendar of Soldier Saints will show:—

CALENDAR OF SOLDIER SAINTS.

(Privileged with many Indulgences by His Holiness Pope Pius IX.)

ST. FLORIAN, PRAY FOR US, THAT WE MAY BE MADE WORTHY OF THE PROMISES OF CHRIST.

PATRON OF THE INFANTRY: S. MAURICE, OF THE THEBAN LEGION.
PATRON OF THE CAVALRY: S. GEORGE.
PATRON OF THE ARTILLERY: S. BARBARA.
PATRON OF THE SAPPERS AND MINERS: S. JOSEPH.

January.

1. 30 Martyrs
2. Marcellinus
3. Gordius
4. Edward King.
7. Canute, King.
12. 40 Martyrs.
13. Godfred & 40 Martyrs
18. Moseus and Ammonius.
20. Sebastian,
28. Charlemagne Emperor
29. Papias and Maurus

February.

2. Cornelius
4. Philoromus
7. Adacavus, Theodore and Richard, Kings
10. 10 Martyrs
12. Damianus
21. Edelbert, King
27. Besa

March.

3. Marinus, Hemite-rius, Cheledonius, Cleomicus, Eutropius and Basiliscus
4. Casimir, Prince
8. John of God
10. 40 Martyrs
15. Longinus
18. Edward, King
20. Sebastian
23. Victorian
27. Alexander Amphilochius and Cronidas
28. Gunthram, King
29. Armogastus
30. 30 Quirinus

April.

11. 8. Martyrs
13. Hermenegild, Prince
16. Gerald, Duke
18. Corebus
23. George
24. Sabas
28. Vitalis
29. Aemilian

May.

1. Sigismund, King
3. Alexander
4. Florian
8. Victor and Acathius
13. Gangolph
18. Soleeamus and his companions; Erich, King
21. Nicostratus and Antiochus and another
24. Meletius and 252 Soldiers
25. Gerlach
27. Julius
28. William Duke
30. Ferdinand, King
31. Hermias

June.

1. Ischyrion and 5 Soldiers, Felinus Gratian Crescentian and Wistan Prince
7. Gottschalk, Prince
12. Basilides, Cyrinus, Nabor and Nazarius
15. Hesychius
17. Montanus
18. Leontius and Hypatius
22. A Soldier, who led S. Alban to Martyrdom. Galenus, Valenus, Achatius, Theodore and 10,000 Martyrs
24. Seven brothers— Orentius, Heros, Pharnacius, Firminus, Firmus, Cyriacus and Longinus
25. Gallican
27. Ladislaus, King
30. Basilides, who led St. Potamiona to Martyrdom.

July.

1. Rumald, Prince
2. 3 Soldiers converted by the death of S. Paulus, the Martyr.
5. William
8. 50 Martyrs
12. John Gaulbert
14. Justus
15. Henry Emp.
18. Camillus de Lellis
20. Hieronimus Aemilianus.
21. Victor Alexander, Felician and Longinus.
23. Victor and 83 Soldiers.
29. Olav, King.
31. Fabius & Ignatius of Loyola.

August.

5. Ensignius and Oswald, King
7. Faustus and Victricius
9. Romanus.
10. 165 Martyrs.
16. Ambrose and Arsacius.
20. Memnon.
21. Anastasius.
25. Louis, King
26. Secundus and Alexander of the Theban Legion.
27. Marcellinus.
28. Julian.
29. Sebbus, King

September.

2. Stephen, King.
5. Eudoxius, Zeno, Macarius and 104 companions.
8. Adrian.
9. Severian.
14. Cerealis.
18. Ferreolus.
20. Eustache, sometimes called Placidus.
22. Mauritius, Exuperius, Candidus, Victor, Innocentius Vitalis and the holy Martyrs of the Theban Legion.
25. Herculan.
26. Callistratus and 49 Soldiers.
28. Venceslaus, King and 30 Soldiers.
30. Victor, Ursus and Antoninus of the Theban Legion.

October.

2. Eleutherius, with innumerable others.
3. Gerhard.
4. Thyrsus Secundus Boniface and 300 Soldiers.
8. Demetrius.
10. Victor Gereon, Cassius Florentius Mallusius and 957

	October.		November.		
	companions of the Theb. Legion.	1.	All Saints.	25.	Mercurius.
13.	Edward, King and Gerald.	3.	Hubertus.		**December.**
15.	Maurus.	9.	Theodore.		
19.	Varus.	10.	Respicius and Quintinus.	3.	Claudius and 70 Soldiers.
20.	Artemius.	11.	Martinus and Mennas.	5.	Lucius, King.
21.	Dasius, Zoticus Cajus and 12 Soldiers.	15.	Leopold, Count of the March.	7.	Agatho.
				16.	Valentine.
				18.	Auxentius.
22.	Heraclius.	18.	Hesychus.	20.	Ammon, Zeno, Ptolomaeus Ingenes and Theophilus.
25.	Theodosius, Lucius Marcus, Petrus, Miniates and 46 Soldiers.	19.	Azu and 150 Soldiers.		
		20.	Octavius, Solutor and Adventor of the Theb. Legion, and Edmund, King.	22.	Flavian, Zeno,
27.	Eelasbaan, King.			26.	Commemoration of all Martyrs.
29.	Ferrutius.				
30.	Marcellus.			29.	David, King.

His Holiness Pope Pius IX, on the 9th April 1862, granted the following indulgences—

1. An indulgence of 100 days to all those, who devoutly recite one "Our Father" and one "Hail Mary" for the soldiers, that they may lead a Christian life, valiantly resisting the temptations of the world.

2. A plenary indulgence to those, who with the above intention recite daily during a whole month, one "Our Father and one "Hail Mary," and worthily receive once a month the Sacrament of Penance and Holy Communion.

3. A plenary indulgence to those, who with the above intention receive worthily the Sacraments of Penance and the Holy Eucharist on the following feasts; Blessed Virgin of Victory (1st Sunday in October); St. Michael the Archangel (29th September) St. Joseph (19th March), St. Florian (4th May, St. Barbara (4th December).

IMPRIMATUR.

✠ LEO MEURIN, S. J.

Epus. Vicarius Apostolicus Bomb. & Poonensis.

Bombaii 8a Aprilis 1874.

Of those holy soldiers who are generally more known, Alban Butler in his Lives of the Saints gives very interesting particulars, which you may read with profit and edification in the following pages.

January 20.

St. Sebastian.

St. Sebastian was a captain in a company of the Pretorian guards, an office attended with a very considerable dignity. When under the Emperor Dioclesian, in the year 286, the persecution grew hot, Pope Caius selected Sebastian to stay in Rome to defend the Church, by encouraging and otherwise assisting the martyrs. He acquitted himself of this arduous and dangerous duty admirably, until at length he was himself accused of being a Christian and brought before the Emperor Dioclesian, who sentenced him to be shot by certain archers of Mauritania. His body was pierced all over with arrows, and he was left for dead. But a Christian woman who went to bury him found him still alive, took him to her home, where through her care he recovered, but refused to fly, and even placed himself one day on a staircase where the Emperor was to pass. When the latter had come up to where he stood, he reproached him for his cruelties against the Christians. The freedom of speech from a person, whom he supposed to have been dead, greatly affected the Emperor; but recovering from his consternation, he gave orders for his being seized and beaten to death with cudgels, and his body thrown into the common sewer. A pious lady, called Lucina, admonished by the martyr in a vision, got it privately removed and buried. His relics are still kept in Belgium, France and Germany, and St. Sebastian has been always honoured by the Church as one of her most illustrious martyrs. By praying to him, Rome was freed from a raging pestilence in 680, Milan in 1575, Lisbon in 1599, and other places have experienced, in like calamities, the miraculous effects of his intercession with God on their behalf.

March 10.
The Forty Martyrs of Sebaste.
A. D. 320.

These holy martyrs suffered at Sebaste in the Lesser Armenia, under the Emperor Licinius, in 320. They were of different countries, but enrolled in the same troop, all in the flower of their age, comely, brave, and robust, and were become considerable for their services. St. Gregory of Nyssa and Procopius say, they were of the thundering legion, so famous under Marcus Aurelius for the miraculous rain and victory obtained by their prayers. This was the twelfth legion then quartered in Armenia. Lysias was duke or general of the forces, and Agricola the governor of the Province. The latter having signified to the army the orders of the Emperor Licinius, for all to sacrifice, these forty went boldly up to him, and said they were Christians, and that no torments should make them ever abandon their holy religion. The judge first endeavoured to gain them by mild usage, as, by representing to them the dishonour that would attend their refusal to do what was required, and by making them large promises of preferment and high favour with the Emperor in case of compliance. Finding these methods of gentleness ineffectual, he had recourse to threats, and these the most terrifying, if they continued disobedient to the Emperor's order, but all in vain. To his promises they answered that he could give them nothing equal to what he would deprive them of ; and to his threats, that his power only extended over their bodies, which they had learned to despise when their souls were at stake. The governor finding them all resolute caused them to be torn with whips, and their sides to be rent with iron-hooks. After which they were loaded with chains, and committed to jail.

After some days, Lysias their general coming from Cæsarea to Sebaste they were re-examined, and no less generously rejected the large promises made them, than they despised the torments they were threatened with. The governor, highly offended at their courage and that liberty of speech with which they accosted him, devised an extraordinary kind of death, which being slow and severe, he hoped would shake their constancy. The cold in Armenia is very sharp, especially in March, and towards the end of winter, when the wind is north, as it then was, there being also at that time a severe frost. Under the walls of the town stood a pond which was frozen so hard that it would bear walking upon with safety. The judge ordered the saints to be exposed quite naked on the ice. And in order to tempt them the more powerfully to renounce their faith, a warm bath was prepared at a small distance from the frozen pond, for any of the company to go to, who were disposed to purchase their temporal ease and safety on that condition. The martyrs, on hearing their sentence, ran joyfully to the place, and without waiting to be stripped, undressed themselves, encouraging one another in the same manner as is usual among soldiers in military expeditions attended with hardships and dangers, saying, that one bad night would purchase them a happy eternity. They also made this their joint prayers: "Lord, we are forty who are engaged in this combat, grant that we may be forty crowned, and that not one be wanting to this sacred number." The guards in the mean time ceased not to persuade them to sacrifice, that by so doing they might be allowed to pass to the warm bath. But, though it is not easy to form a just idea of the bitter pain they must have undergone, of the whole number only one had the misfortune to be overcome; who losing courage went off from the pond to seek the relief in readiness for such as were disposed to renounce their faith: but as the devil usually deceives his adorers, the apostate no sooner entered the warm water than he expired. This misfortune afflicted the martyrs; but they were quickly comforted by seeing his place and their number miraculously filled up. A sentinel was warming himself near the bath, having been posted there to observe if any of the martyrs were inclined to submit. While he was attending, he had a vision of blessed spirits descending from heaven on the martyrs, and distributing, as from their king, rich presents and precious garments, Saint Ephrem adds, crowns, to all these generous soldiers, one only excepted, who was their faint-hearted companion, already mentioned. The guard being struck with the celestial vision and the apostate's desertion was converted upon it, and by a particular motion of the Holy Ghost, threw off his clothes, and placed himself in his stead amongst the thirty-nine martyrs. Thus God heard their request, though in another manner than they imagined: "Which ought to make us adore the impenetrable secrets of his mercy and justice," says St. Ephrem, "in this instance, no less than in the reprobation of Judas, and the election of St. Matthias."

In the morning the judge ordered both those that were dead with the cold, and those that were still alive to be laid on carriages, and cast into a fire. When the rest were thrown into a waggon to be carried to the pile, the youngest of them (whom the acts call Melita) was found alive, and the executioners hoping he would change his resolution when he came to himself, left him behind. His mother, a woman of mean condition, and a widow, but rich in faith and worthy to have a son, a martyr, observing this false compassion, reproached the executioners; and when she came up to her son, whom she found quite frozen, not able to stir, and scarce breathing, he looked on her with languishing eyes, and made a little sign with his weak hand to comfort her. She exhorted him to persevere to the end, and fortified by the Holy Ghost, took him up and put him with her own hands into the waggon with the rest of the martyrs, not only without shedding a tear, but with a countenance full of joy, saying courageously: "Go, go, son, proceed to the end of this happy journey with thy companions that thou mayest not be the last of them that shall present themselves before God." Nothing can be more inflamed or more pathetic than the discourse which St. Ephrem puts into her mouth, by which he expresses her contempt of life and all earthly things, and her ardent love and desire of eternal life. This holy Father earnestly entreats her to conjure this whole troop of martyrs to join in imploring the divine mercy in favour of his sinful soul. Their bodies were burned and their ashes thrown into the river, but the Christians secretly carried off or purchased part of them with money. Some of these precious relics were kept at Cæsarea, and St. Basil says of them: "Like bulwarks they are our protection against the inroads of enemies." He adds, that every one implored their succour, and that they raised up those that had fallen, strengthened the weak, and invigorated the fervour of the Saints.

April 23.

Saint George Martyr.

A. D. 302.

St. George is honoured in the Catholic Church as one of the most illustrious martyrs of Christ. The Greeks have long distinguished him by the title of the Great Martyr, and keep his festival a holiday of obligation. There stood formerly in Constantinople five or six churches dedicated in his honour, the oldest of which was always said to have been built by Constantine the Great, who seems also to have been the founder of the Church of St. George, which stood over his tomb in Palestine.

One of the churches of St. George in Constantinople called Manganes, with a monastery adjoining, gave to the Hellespont the name of the *Arm of St. George*. To this day St. George is honoured as principal patron or tutelar Saint by several eastern nations particularly the Georgians. The Byzantine historians relate several battles to have been gained, and other miracles wrought through his intercession. From frequent pilgrimages to his church and tomb in Palestine performed by those who visited the Holy Land, his veneration was much propagated over the West. St. Gregory of Tours mentions him as highly celebrated in France in the sixth century.

The intercession of this Saint was implored especially in battles, and by warriors, as appears by several instances in the Byzantine history and he is said to have been himself a great soldier. He is at this day the tutelar Saint of the republic of Genoa; and was chosen by our ancestors in the same quality under our first Norman Kings. The great national council held at Oxford in 1222, commanded his feast to be kept a holiday of the lesser rank throughout all England. Under his name an ensign was instituted by our victorious King Edward III in 1330, the most noble order of knighthood in Europe, consisting of twenty-five knights, besides the Sovereign. The extraordinary devotion of all Christendom to this Saint, is an authentic proof of how glorious his triumph and name have always been in the Church. All his acts relate that he suffered under Dioclesian at Nicomedia. Joseph Assemani shows, from the unanimous consent of all churches, that he was crowned on the 23rd of April. According to the account given us by Metaphrastes, he was born in Capadocia of noble Christian parents. After the death of his father, he went with his mother into Palestine, she being a native of that country, and having there a considerable estate, which fell to her son George. He was strong and robust in body, and having embraced the profession of a soldier, was made a tribune, or colonel in the army. By his courage and conduct he was soon preferred to higher stations by the Emperor Dioclesian. When that prince waged war against the Christian religion, St. George laid aside the marks of his dignity. threw up his commission and posts, and complained to the Emperor himself of his severities and bloody edicts. He was immediately cast into prison, and tried, first by promises, and afterwards tortured with great cruelty; but nothing could shake his constancy. The next day he was led through the city and beheaded.

The reason why St. George has been regarded as the patron of military men, is partly upon the score of his profession, and partly upon the credit of his appearing to the Christian army in the holy war, before the battle of Antioch. The success of this battle proving fortunate to the Christians, under Godfrey of Bouillon, made the name of St. George more famous in Europe, and disposed the military men to implore more particularly his intercession. This devotion was confirmed, as it is said, by an apparition of St. George to our King Richard I in his expedition against the Saracens: which vision being declared to the troops, was to them a great encouragement, and they soon after defeated the enemy. St. George is usually painted on horse-back, and tilting at a dragon, under his feet: but this representation is no more than an emblematical figure, purporting, that by his faith and Christian fortitude, he conquered the devil, called the dragon in the Apocalypse.

May 14.

St. Pachomius, Abbot.

A. D. 348.

He was born in Upper Thebais about the year 292, of idolatrous parents, and was educated in their blind superstition, and in the study of the Egyptian sciences. From his infancy he was meek and modest, and had an aversion to the profane ceremonies used by the infidels in the worship of their idols. Being about twenty years of age, he was pressed into the Emperor's troops, probably the tyrant Maximinus, who was master of Egypt from the year 310, and in 312 made great levies to carry out a war against Licinius and Constantine. He was, with several other recruits, put on board a vessel that was sailing down the river. They arrived in the evening at Thebes or Diospolis, the capital of Thebais, a city in which dwelt many Christians. Those true disciples of Christ sought every opportunity of relieving and comforting all that were in distress, and were moved with compassion towards the recruits who were kept close confined and very ill-treated. The Christians of this city showed them the same tenderness as if they had been their own children; took all possible care of them, and supplied them liberally with money and necessaries. Such an uncommon example of disinterested virtue made a great impression on the mind of Pachomius. He inquired who their pious benefactors were, and when he heard that they believed in Jesus Christ the only Son of God, and that in hope of a reward in the world to come they laboured continually to do good to all mankind. he found kindled in his heart a great love of so holy a law, and an ardent desire of serving the God whom these good men adored. The next day, when he was continuing his journey down the river, the remembrance of this purpose strengthened him to resist a carnal temptation. From his infancy he had always been a lover of chastity and temperance, but the example of the Christians had made those virtues appear to him far more amiable, and in a new light. After the overthrow of Maximinus, his forces were disbanded. Pachomius had no sooner returned home, but he repaired to a town in Thebais, in which there was a Christian church, and there he entered his name among the catechumens, or such as were preparing for baptism; and having gone through the usual course of preliminary instructions and practices with great attention and fervour, he received the sacrament at Chenoboscium, with great sentiments of devotion and piety. From his first acquaintance with our holy faith at Thebes, he had always made this his prayer: " O God, Creator of heaven and earth, cast on me an eye of pity: deliver me from my miseries: teach me the true way of pleasing you, and it shall be the whole employment, and most earnest study of my life to serve you, and to do your will." The perfect sacrifice of his heart to God was the beginning of his eminent virtue. The grace by which God reigns in a soul, is a treasure infinitely above all price. We must give all to purchase it. To desire it faintly is to undervalue it. He is absolutely disqualified and unfit for so great a blessing and unworthy ever to receive it, who seeks it by halves, or who does not esteem all other things as dung that he may gain Christ. When Pachomius was baptized, he began seriously to consider with himself how he should most faithfully fulfil the obligations which he had contracted, and attain to the great end to which he aspired. There is danger even in fervour itself. It is often an artifice of the devil to make a novice undertake too much at first, and run indiscreetly beyond his strength. If the sails gather too much wind, the vessel is driven a-head, falls on some rock and splits. Eagerness is a symptom of secret passion not of true virtue, where it is wilful and impatient of advice. Pachomius was far from so dangerous a disposition, because his desire was pure, therefore his first care was to find a skilful conductor. Hearing that a venerable old man named Palemon served God in the desert in great perfection, he sought him out, and with great earnestness begged to live under his direction. The hermit having set before him the difficulties and austerities of his way of life, which several had already attempted in vain to follow, advised him to make a trial of his strength and fervour in some monastery; and, to give him a sketch of the great difficulties he had to encounter in the life he aspired to, he added: "Consider, my son, that my diet is only bread and salt: I drink no wine, use no oil, watch one half of the night, spending that time in singing psalms or in meditating on the holy Scriptures, and sometimes pass the whole night without sleeping." Pachomius was amazed at this account, but not discouraged. He thought himself able to undertake everything that might be a means to render his soul pleasing to God, and readily promised to observe whatever Palemon should think fit to enjoin on him, who therefore admitted him into his cell, and gave him the monastic habit. Pachomius was by his example enabled to bear solitude, and an acquaintance with himself. They sometimes repeated together the psalter, at other times they exercised themselves in manual labours, (which they accompanied with interior prayers) with a view to their own subsistence and the relief of the poor. Pachomius prayed above all things for perfect purity of heart, that being disengaged from all secret attachment to creatures, he might love God with all his affections. And to destroy the very roots of all inordinate passions, it was his first study to obtain the most profound humility, and perfect patience and meekness. He prayed often with his arms stretched out in the form of a cross, which posture was then much used in the church. He was in the beginning often drowsy at the night office. Palemon used to rouse him, and say: Labour and watch my dear Pachomius, lest the enemy overthrow you and ruin all your endeavours." Against this weakness and temptation he enjoined him, on such occasions, to carry sand from one place to another till his drowsiness was overcome. By this means the novice strengthened himself in the habit of watching. Whatever instructions he read or heard, he immediately endeavoured fervently to reduce to practice. One Easter-day Palemon bade the disciple prepare a dinner for that great festival. Pachomius took a little oil and mixed it with the salt which he pounded well, and added a few wild herbs, which they were to eat with their bread. The holy old man having made his prayer, came to table but at the sight of the oil he struck himself on the forehead, and said with tears: " My Saviour was crucified, and shall I indulge so far as to eat oil?" Nor could he be prevailed upon to taste it. Pachomius used sometimes to go into a vast uninhabited desert, on the banks of the Nile, called Tabenna, in the diocese of Tentyra, a city between the Great and Little Diospolis. Whilst he was there one day in prayer, he heard a voice which commanded him to build a monastery in that place, in which he should receive those who should be sent by God to serve Him faithfully. He received, about the same time, from an angel who appeared to him, certain instructions relating to a monastic life. Pachomius going back to Palemon, imparted to him this vision; and both of them coming to Tabenna built there a little cell towards the year 325. He died when 57 years old the death of a Saint.

May 27.

St. Julius, M.

This martyr was a *veteran soldier*, and was impeached by his officers for the Christian faith, before Maximus, governor of the Lower Mœsia, which was afterwards called Bulgaria. Pasicrates and Valention, both of the same regiment, had received the crown of martyrdom a little before. The judge employed caresses, promises and threats; but Julius professed that to die for Christ in order to live eternally with him would be the accomplishment of all his desires. Whereupon he was condemned to lose his head, and led forth to the place of execution. As he went, Hesychius, a Christian soldier, who was also a prisoner and suffered martyrdom a few days after him, said: "Go with courage, and run to the crown which the Lord hath promised; and remember me who shall shortly follow you. Commend me to the servants of God, Pasicrates and Valention, who by confessing the holy name of Jesus are gone before us."

Julius embracing Hesychius said: "Dear brother, make haste to come to us; they whom you salute have already heard you. Julius bound his eyes with a handkerchief, and presenting his neck to the executioner, said: "Lord Jesus, for whose name I suffer death, vouchsafe to receive my soul in the number of thy Saints." His martyrdom happened on the 27th of May, two days after that of St. Pasicrates, about the year 302, in the reign of Dioclesian, at Durostoro on the Danube.

June 12.

S. S. Basilides, Cuirinus or Cyrinus, Nabor and Nazarius, Martyrs.

Saints Gelasius and Gregory the Great in their Sacramentaries, the ancient Roman Calendar, make honourable mention of these four martyrs who suffered at Rome, and were interred on the Aurelian road. According to the Acts of Martyrdom, they were *four soldiers* in the army of Maxentius, son of Maximian Herculius, and after suffering many torments were beheaded by the command of Aurelius, prefect of Rome.

July 20.

St. Jerom of Aemilian, C.

Founder of the Congregation of Regular Clergy of Somascha.

He was born at Venice of a patrician family and in the most troublesome times of the Republic, *served in the troops from his childhood.* Whilst he was governor of the new castle in the mountains of Tarviso, he was taken prisoner, cast into a dungeon, and loaded with chains. His sufferings he sanctified by penance and prayer, and being delivered by the miraculous protection of the Mother of God, arriving at Tarviso, he hung up his chains before an altar consecrated to God under the invocation of the Blessed Virgin, and, returning to Venice, devoted himself to the exercises of prayer and all virtues.

At that time a famine and a contagious distemper having reduced many families to the greatest distress, he laid himself out in relieving all, but was particularly moved with compassion for abandoned orphans. These he gathered in a house which he hired, clothed and fed them at his own expense, and instructed them himself with unwearied zeal in the Christian doctrine and in all virtues. By the advice of St. Cajetan and others he passed to the Continent and erected little hospitals for orphans at Brescia, Bergamo, and other places, and others for the reception of penitent women. At Somascha on the frontiers of the Venetian dominions between Bergamo and Milan, he founded a house which he destined for the exercises of those whom he received into his Congregation, and in which he long resided. From this house it took its name, though it was sometimes called St. Mayeul's, titular of a college at Pavia, which St. Charles Borromeo put under his direction.

The instruction of youth and young clergymen became also an object of his zeal in his foundations, and continues still to be in this Institute. The brothers, during the life of the founder, were all laymen, and it was only approved as a pious Congregation. The holy founder died at Somascha on the 8th of February, 1537, of a contagious distemper which he had caught by attending the sick. He was beatified by Benedict XIV and canonized by Clement XIII. An office in his honour was appointed for the 20th of July, by a decree of the Holy See published in 1769.

July 21.

St. Victor of Marseilles M.

The emperor Maximian, reeking with the blood of the Theban legion and many other martyrs whom he had massacred in different parts of Gaul, arrived at Marseilles the most numerous and flourishing church in those provinces. The tyrant breathed here nothing but slaughter and fury, and his coming filled the Christians with fear and alarms. In this general consternation, Victor, a Christian officer in the troops, went about in the night from house to house visiting the faithful and inspiring them with contempt of a temporal death and the love of eternal life. He was surprised in this action, so worthy a soldier of Jesus Christ, and brought before the prefects Asterius and Eutychius, who exhorted him not to lose the fruit of all his services and the favour of his prince for the worship of a dead man, so they called Jesus Christ. He answered, that he renounced those recompenses if he could not enjoy them without being unfaithful to Jesus Christ, the eternal Son of God, who vouchsafed to become man for our salvation, but who raised himself from the dead, and reigns with the Father, being God equally with him. The whole court heard him with tumultuous shouts of indignation and rage. However the prisoner being a person of distinction, the prefects sent him to Maximian himself. The incensed countenance of an emperor did not daunt the champion of Christ, and the tyrant seeing his threats to have no effect upon him, commanded him to be bound hands and feet and dragged through all the streets of the city, exposed to the blows and insults of the populace. Every one of the heathens seemed to think it a crime not to testify their false zeal by offering some indignity or other to the martyr. Their design was to intimidate the Christians, but the example of the martyr's resolution served to encourage them. Victor was brought back bruised and bloody to the tribunal of the prefects, who thinking his resolution must have been weakened by his sufferings, began to blaspheme our holy religion and pressed him again to adore their gods. But the martyr filled with the Holy Ghost and encouraged by His presence in his soul expressed his respect for the emperor and his contempt of their gods, adding, "I despise your deities, and confess Jesus Christ; inflict upon me what torments you please." The two prefects only disagreed about the choice of the tortures. After a warm contest, Eutychius withdrew and left the prisoner to Asterius, who commanded him to be hoisted on the rack, and most cruelly tortured a long time. The martyr lifting up his eyes to heaven asked patience and constancy of God, whose gifts he knew it to be. Jesus Christ appeared to him on the rack, holding a cross in his hands, gave him his peace, and told him that he suffered in his servants, and crowned them after their victory. These words dispelled both his pains and his grief; and the tormentors being at last weary, the prefect ordered him to be taken down and thrown into a dark dungeon. At midnight God visited him by his angels, the prison was filled with a light brighter than that of the sun, and the martyr sung with the angels the praises of God. Three soldiers, who guarded the prison, seeing this light, were surprised at the miracle, and casting themselves at the martyr's feet, asked his pardon and desired baptism. Their names were Alexander, Longinus, and Felician. The martyr instructed them as well as time would permit, sent for priests the same night, and going with them to the sea-side, he led them out of the water, that is, was their godfather, and returned with them again to his prison.

The next morning Maximian was informed of the conversion of the guards, and, in a transport of rage, sent officers to bring them all four before him in the middle of the market-place. The mob loaded Victor with injuries, and would fain have compelled him to bring back his converts to the worship of their gods, but he said: "I cannot undo what is well done." And turning to them he encouraged them saying:

"You are still soldiers; behave with courage, God will give you victory. You belong to Jesus Christ, be faithful. An immortal crown is prepared for you." The three soldiers persevered in the confession of Jesus Christ, and by the emperor's orders were forthwith beheaded. Victor prayed in the meantime with tears that he might, by being united with them in their happy death, be presented in their glorious company before God; but after having been exposed to the insults of the whole city as an immovable rock lashed with the waves, and been beaten with clubs and scourged with leather-thongs he was carried back to prison, where he continued three days, recommending to God his martyrdom with many tears. After that term the emperor called him again before his tribunal, and having caused a statue of Jupiter with an altar and incense to be placed by him he commanded the martyr to offer incense to the idol. Victor went up to the profane altar, and by a stroke of his foot threw it down. The Emperor ordered the foot to be forthwith chopped off, which the Saint suffered with great joy, offering to God these first fruits of his body. A few moments after, the emperor condemned him to be put under the grindstone of a handmill, and crushed to death. The executioners turned the wheel, and when part of his body was bruised and crushed, the mill broke down. The Saint still breathed a little; but his head was immediately ordered to be cut off. His and the other three bodies were thrown into the sea, but being cast ashore were buried by the Christians in a grotto hewn out of a rock. The author of the acts adds: "they are honoured to this day with many miracles, and many benefits are conferred by God and our Lord Jesus Christ on those who asked them through their merits."

August 9.

St. Romanus, M.

He was a soldier in Rome at the time of the martyrdom of St. Lawrence. Seeing the joy and constancy with which that holy martyr suffered his torments, he was moved to embrace the faith, and addressing himself to St. Lawrence, was instructed and baptized by him in prison. Confessing aloud what he had done, he was arraigned, condemned, and beheaded the day before the martyrdom of St. Lawrence. Thus he arrived at his crown before his guide and master. The body of St. Romanus was first buried on the road to Tibur, but his remains were translated to Lucca, where they are kept under the high altar of a beautiful church which bears his name.

August 28.

St. Julian. M.

He was descended from one of the best families of Vienne in Dauphiné. He served with the tribune

Ferreol, and knew well how to reconcile the profession of arms with the maxims of the gospel. Crispin, governor of the province of Vienne, having declared himself against the Christians, our Saint withdrew to Auvergne, not that he dreaded the persecution but that he might be at hand to be of service to the faithful, for being acquainted that he was sought after by the persecutors, of his own accord he presented himself before them saying, "Alas, I am too long in this bad world; oh! how I burn with desire to be with Jesus." He had scarce uttered these words, when they separated his head from his body. It was near Brioude; but the place of his interment was for a long time unknown, until God revealed it to St. Germain of Auxerre, when he passed by Brioude on his return from Arles about the year 431. His head was afterwards translated to Vienne with the body of St. Ferreol. St. Gregory of Tours relates a great number of miracles wrought by his intercession. The same author mentions a church dedicated at Paris under the invocation of the holy martyr, it is that which is near the bridge called Petit pont, and has successively gone under the name of St. Julian the Old, and St. Julian the Poor.

September 8.
St. Adrian, M.

This saint was an *officer in the Roman army*, who having persecuted the Christians in the reign of

Maximian Galerius, was so moved by their constancy and patience that he embraced their faith, and suffered many torments and a glorious martyrdom for the same, at Nicomedia, about the year 306 in the tenth or last general persecution. His relics were conveyed to Constantinople, thence to Rome, afterward into Flanders, where they were deposited in the Benedictine Abbey of Decline dedicated in honour of St. Peter.

September 18.

St. Ferreol, M.

St. Ferreol was a *Colonel*, lived at Vienne in Gaul, and was secretly a Christian. St. Julian of Brioude, a native of that city and a person of high birth lodged in his house, and made public profession of the Christian faith. When the persecution began to rage St. Julian withdrew into Auvergne, and lay some time concealed in the house of a widow at Vinicelle near the town of Brioude. Certain pursuivants having got information about him, the servant of Christ discovered himself to them, that the widow who had concealed him might not be brought into danger. The soldiers cut off his head upon the spot and carried it back with them to Vienne that his execution might strike a terror into the rest of the Christians. Crispin, governor of that part of Gaul, caused St. Ferreol to be apprehended upon suspicion. Finding him refuse to offer sacrifice, he told him that as he had the honour to serve his country in so eminent a station, it became him to set an example of obedience. The martyr answered: "I do not so much overrate the honours and riches which I enjoy. If I may be allowed to live and to serve God, I am well satisfied; if even this seems too much, I am willing to resign my life itself rather than to abandon my religion." The judge commanded that he should be scourged, and then laid in the dungeon loaded with chains. On the third day after this his chains fell off his hands and legs, and seeing the door of the prison open and his guards asleep, he made his escape, and went out of the city by the gate which led to Lyons. He swam over the river Rhone, and got as far as the river Geres, which falls into the Rhone two leagues above Vienne when he fell again into the hands of the persecutors, who tied his hands behind his back, and led him part of the way with them, till being seized with a sudden fit of savage cruelty, they cut off his head near the banks of the Rhone about the year 304. The Christians of Vienne interred his body with great veneration near the same river, and the citizens experience his protection by frequent benefits which they receive from God through the prayers which they perform at his tomb.

September 22.
St. Maurice and his Companions.
A. D. 286.

The emperor Carus, who had impiously assumed the title of a god, being killed by lightning, and his son Numerianus Augustus being cut off by the treachery of his uncle Aper, Dioclesian, a man of low birth, was saluted emperor by the army, which he then commanded in the East, on the 17th September, 284. He defeated and slew Carinus, the second debauched son of Carus the year following in Moesia, and after this victory took the haughty name of Jovius from Jupiter, and, creating Maximian Cæsar, allotted to him the care and defence of the West. The Bagaudal, a people, consisting chiefly of peasants in Gaul who had been attached to the interest of Carinus, took up arms to revenge his death under two commanders Amandus and Ælian. Dioclesian ordered Maximian to march against them, and on that occasion declared him Augustus and partner in the empire, and this new emperor assumed the surname of Hercules. In this expedition the most judicious historians place the martyrdom of the Theban legion. It seems to have received its name from being raised in Thebais or Upper Egypt, a country full of zealous Christians. This legion was entirely composed of such; and St. Maurice, who seems to have been the first commanding officer that was then with it, made it a point to admit no others among them.

Dioclesian in the beginning of his reign was no enemy to the Christian religion, and employed many, who openly professed it, near his own person, and in posts of trust and importance, as Eusebius assures us. Yet even private governors and the giddy populace were at liberty to indulge the blindest passion and fury against the servants of Christ; and Maximian. on certain extraordinary occasions, stained his progresses with the blood of many martyrs. The Theban legion was one of those which were sent by Dioclesian out of the East to compose his army for his expedition into Gaul. Maximian in crossing the Alps made a halt with his army some days, that the soldiers might repose themselves in their tedious march while some detachments filed off towards Triers. They were then arrived at Octodurum, at that time a considerable city on the Rhone. Here Maximian issued out an order that the whole army should join in offering sacrifice to the gods for the success of their expedition. The Theban legion hereupon withdrew itself and encamped near Agaunum, now called St. Maurice, three leagues from Octodurum. The emperor sent them repeated orders to return to the camp and join in the sacrifices, and upon their constant and unanimous refusal he commanded them to be decimated. Thus every tenth man was put to death. according as the lot fell; the rest exhorting one another all the while to perseverance. After the first decimation, a second was commanded, unless the soldiers obeyed the order given, but they cried out over their whole camp that they would rather suffer all extremities than do anything contrary to their holy religion. They were principally encouraged by three of their general officers, Maurice or Mauritius, Exuperius, and Candidus. St. Eucherius does not style St. Maurice the tribune, but Primicerius, which was the dignity of the first captain, next to that of the tribune or colonel. He calls Exuperius Campiductor or Major, and Candidus the senator of the troops.

The emperor sent fresh threats, that it was in vain they confided in their multitude; and that if they persisted in their disobedience not a man among them should escape death. The legion, by the advice of their generous leaders, answered him by a dutiful remonstrance, the substance of which was as follows: " We are your soldiers, but are servants of the true God. We owe you military service and obedience; but we cannot renounce him who is our Creator and Master, and also yours, even whilst you reject him. In all things which are not against his law, we most willingly obey you, as we have done hitherto. We readily oppose all your enemies whoever they are, but we cannot dip our hands in the blood of innocent persons. We have taken an oath to God before we took one to you; you can place no confidence in our second oath, should we violate the first. You command us to punish the Christians: behold, we are all such. We confess God the Father, Author of all things, and his Son, Jesus Christ. We have seen our companions slain without lamenting them; and we rejoice at their honour. Neither this extremity to which we are reduced nor any provocation hath tempted us to revolt. We have arms in our hands, but we do not resist, because we had rather die innocent than live by any sin."

This legion consisted of about six thousand six hundred men, who were all armed, and might have sold their lives very dear. But they had learned to give to God what is God's, and to Cæsar what is Cæsar's, and they showed their courage more in dying than they had ever done in the most hazardous enterprises. Maximian, having no hopes of overcoming their constancy, commanded his whole army to surround them, and cut them to pieces. They made no resistance, but, dropping their arms, suffered themselves to be butchered like innocent sheep without opening their mouths, except mutually to encourage one another; and not one out of so great a number failed in courage to the last. The ground was covered with their dead bodies, and streams of blood flowed on every side. Maximian gave the spoils of the slain to his army for their booty, and the soldiers were making merry over them, when Victor, a veteran soldier, who belonged not to that troop, happened to pass by. They invited him to eat with them, but he, detesting their feast,

offered to retire. At this the soldiers inquired if
he was also a Christian. He answered that he was,
and would always continue one : upon which they
instantly fell upon him and slew him. Ursus and
Victor, two straggling soldiers of this legion, were
found at Solodora, now Soleure, and massacred upon
the spot. Their relics are still preserved at Soleure.
These martyrs were styled by Fortunatus : " The
happy legion."

October 30.

St. Marcellus the Centurion, Martyr.

A. D. 298.

The birthday of the emperor Maximian Herculeus
was celebrated in the year 298 with extraordinary
feasting and solemnity. Pompous sacrifices to the
Roman gods made a considerable part of this solemnity.
Marcellus, a Christian *centurion or captain in
the legion of Trajan*, then posted in Spain, not to
defile himself with taking part in those impious abominations,
cast away his military belt at the head
of his company, declaring aloud that he was a *soldier
of Jesus Christ*, the eternal King. He also threw
down his arms and the vine-branch, which was the
mark of his post of centurion—for the Roman
officers were forbidden to strike a soldier with any
instrument except a vine-branch which the centurions

usually carried in their hands. The soldiers informed Anastasius Fortunatus, prefect of the legion, by whose order Marcellus was committed to prison. When the festival was over, this judge ordered Marcellus to be brought before him, and asked him what he meant by his late proceedings. Marcellus said, "When you celebrated the emperor's festival, I said aloud, that I was a Christian, and could serve no other than Jesus Christ, the Son of God." Fortunatus told him that it was not in his power to connive at his rashness, and that he was obliged to lay his case before the emperors Maximian and Constantius Cæsar. Spain was immediately subject to Constantius, who was at that time Cæsar, and most favourable to the Christians. But Marcellus was sent under a strong guard to Aurelian Agricolaus, vicar to the prefect of the praetorium, who was then at Tangier, in Africa. Agricolaus asked him whether he had really done as the judge's letter set forth; and, upon his confessing the fact, the vicar passed sentence of death upon him for desertion and impiety as he called his action. St. Marcellus was forthwith led to execution and beheaded on the 30th of October. His relics were afterwards translated from Tangier to Leon in Spain, and are kept in a rich shrine in the chief parish church in that city, of which he is the titular saint.

November 9.

Saint Theodorus, surnamed Tyro. M.

St. Gregory of Nyssa begins the panegyric which he pronounced upon this martyr on his festival, at his tomb near Amasea, by gratefully ascribing to his intercession the preservation of that country from the inroads of the Scythians who had laid waste all the neighbouring provinces. Imploring his patronage, he says: "As a soldier defend us; as a martyr speak for us—ask peace: if we want a stronger intercession, gather together your brother martyrs, and with them all pray for us; stir up Peter, Paul, and John, that they be solicitous for the churches which they founded. May no heresies sprout up; may the Christian commonwealth become, by your and your companions' prayers, a flourishing field." The panegyrist testifies, that, by his intercession, devils were expelled, and distempers cured; that many resorted to his church, and admired the stateliness of the buildings, and the actions of the Saint painted on the wall; approached the tomb, being persuaded that the touch thereof imparted a blessing; that they carried the dust of the sepulchre as a treasure of great value, and if any were allowed the happiness to touch the sacred relics, they respectfully applied them to their eyes, mouth, ears, and other organs of their senses. "Then," says the same St. Gregory, shedding tears of devotion, "they address themselves to the martyr as if he were present, and pray and invoke him, who is before God, and obtains gifts as he pleases." The venerable panegyrist procceds to give a short account of the martyr's triumph.

Theodorus was a native of Armenia, young and *newly enlisted in the Roman army* whence he was surnamed Tyro. With his legion he was sent into winter quarters in Pontus, and was at Amasea when fresh edicts were published by Maximian Galerius and Maximin, for continuing with the utmost rigour the persecution which had been raised by Dioclesian. Our young soldier was so far from concealing his faith, that he seemed to carry it written on his forehead. Being seized and presented to the governor of the province and the tribune of his legion, he was asked by them how he dared to profess a religion which the Emperor punished with death? To whom he boldly made the following declaration:—" I know not your gods. Jesus Christ, the only Son of God, is my God. Beat, tear, or burn me, and if my words offend you, cut out my tongue; every part of my body is ready when God calls for it as a sacrifice." His judges, with a pretended compassion for his youth, allowed him time to give the affair a second thought, and dismissed him for the present. Theodorus employed the interval in prayer for perseverance, and being resolved to convince his judges that his resolution was inflexible, by an extraordinary impulse he set fire to a temple of Cybele, which stood upon the banks of the river Tris in the middle of the city, and the fabric was reduced to ashes. When he was carried a second time before the governor and his assistant, he was ready to prevent their questions by his confession. They endeavoured to terrify him with threats of torments, and allure him by promising to make him the priest of the goddess if he would offer sacrifice. His answer was, that their priests were of all idolaters the most miserable, because the most criminal. His body was unmercifully torn with whips, and afterwards hoisted on the rack. Under all manner of torments the Saint maintained his former tranquillity and greatness of soul, and seemingly insensible to the smart of his wounds, ceased not to repeat those words of the Psalmist: "I will bless the Lord at all times: his praises shall be always in my mouth." When the governor's cruelty was tired, the martyr was remanded to prison, where in the night he was wonderfully comforted by God and His holy Angels. After a third examination, Theodorus was condemned to be burnt alive in a furnace; which sentence was executed in the year 306, probably on the 17th February on which day the Greeks and Muscovites celebrate his festival, though the Latins keep it on the 9th of November. The body of this Martyr was translated in the twelfth century to Brindisi, and is there enshrined, except the head, which is at Cajeta.

November 11.

St. Martin, A. D. 397.

The great St. Martin, the glory of Gaul, and the light of the Western Church in the fourth age, was a native of Sabaria, a town of Upper Pannonia, the ruins of which appear upon the river Gunez, in Lower Hungary, two leagues from Sarwar, upon the Raab, near the confines of Austria and Styria. St. Gregory of Tours places his birth in the year 316, or before Easter in 317, the eleventh of Constantine the Great. His parents carried him with them in his infancy to Pavia in Italy, whither they removed, and the saint had his education in that city. His father was an officer in the army, and rose to the commission of a military tribune, not much different from that of a colonel or rather of a brigadier amongst us. Our saint seemed animated from his infancy with the spirit of God, and to have no relish for anything but for His service, though his parents were idolaters. At ten years of age he made his way to the Church against the will of his parents, and desired to be enrolled amongst the catechumens. His request was granted, and he assisted as often as possible at the instructions that were given to such at the church, by which he conceived so ardent a love of God, that at twelve years of age he wished to retire into the desert, and would have done it, had not the tenderness of his age hindered him. His heart, however, was always set upon the Church and monasteries. An imperial order being issued to oblige the sons of veteran officers and soldiers to bear arms, the Saint's own father, who very much desired that his son should follow that profession, discovered him, and at fifteen years of age he was compelled to *take the military oath and was entered in the cavalry.* He contented himself with one servant, and him he treated as if he were his equal: they ate together, and the master frequently performed for him the lowest offices. At the time he remained in the army, he kept himself free from those vices which too frequently sully and degrade that profession, and by his virtue, goodness, and charity, gained the love and esteem of all his companions. He was humble and patient above what human nature seemed capable of, though he was not yet baptized. He comforted all those that suffered affliction, and relieved the distressed, reserving to himself out of his pay only what was sufficient for his daily support.

Of his compassion and charity St. Sulpicius has recorded the following illustrious example:—One day in the midst of a very hard winter and severe frost, when many perished with cold, as he was marching with other officers and soldiers, he met at the gate of the city of Amiens a poor man, almost naked, trembling and shaking for cold, and begging alms of those that passed by. Martin seeing those that went before him take no notice of this miserable object, thought he was reserved for himself; by his charities to others he had nothing left but his arms and clothes upon his back; when, drawing his sword, he cut his cloak into two pieces, gave one to the beggar, and wrapped himself in the other half. Some of the bystanders laughed at the figure he made in that dress, whilst others were ashamed not to have relieved the poor man.

In the following night St. Martin saw in his sleep Jesus Christ dressed in that half of the garment which he had given away, and was bid to look at it well, and asked whether he knew it. He then heard Jesus say to a group of angels that surrounded him: "Martin, yet a catechumen, has clothed me with this garment." This vision inspired the Saint with fresh ardour, and determined him speedily to receive baptism, which he did in the eighteenth year of his age, but still continued almost two years in the army at the request of his tribune, with whom he lived in the most intimate friendship, and who promised to renounce the world when the term of service and commission in which he was then employed, should be elapsed. During this interval Martin was so entirely taken up with the obligations of his baptism, that he had little more than the name of a soldier, and expressed much impatience at being detained one moment from devoting himself solely to the divine service. Upon an irruption which the Germans made into Gaul, the troops were assembled to march against them, and a donative was distributed amongst the soldiers. Martin thought it would be ungenerous and unjust to receive the donative when he had thoughts of quitting the service. He therefore begged that his donative might be bestowed on some other person, and asked his dismission, that he might give himself up totally to the service of Christ. He was told that it was for fear of the battle that was expected next day that he desired his dismission. Martin, with surprising intrepidity, offered to be placed in the front without arms, saying: "In the name of the Lord Jesus, and protected not by a helmet and buckler, but by the sign of the cross, I will thrust myself into the thickest squadrons of the enemy without fear." That night the barbarians demanded and obtained peace; upon which Martin easily procured leave to retire, after having served in the army about five years, according to the most probable accounts. Afterwards he was ordained Priest and became Bishop. He was above fourscore years old, when God was pleased to put a happy end to his labours.

§ 9.—A modern example of a saintly soldier. Joseph Louis Guerin.

(From his life written by Canon Allard.)

He was a native of Belgium and born in 1838. At the age of 16 he entered the Seminary at Nantes to study for the priesthood.* In 1860 when the insolent aggressions of the revolution against the Holy See moved the faithful of all nations to indignation,

---

* Compare the Preface written by Card. Manning, Bayswater, 1864.

Guérin was carried by the ardour of his devotion to place himself at the feet of Christ's Vicar on earth to give his life for him, if God so willed. He had only received the minor orders, and therefore soldiering was no obstacle to his clerical vocation. In June 1860 he came to Rome. In September he was ordered to active service and mortally wounded during the battte at Castelfidardo. His military career will, though it was short, show us how a soldier's duty in camp may be reconciled with the practices of religion.

The love of order and cleanliness for which he had always been distinguished while at the college followed him to the barracks, and was as conspicuous in his accoutrements as in everything else that belonged to him. He said his beads every day, as well as the little Office of the Blessed Virgin, whenever he could find time. He went to Holy Communion regularly every Sunday, and occasionally several times in the week. He employed his leisure hours in visiting the religious monuments of Rome. His piety, cheerfulness, and charity made him esteemed and loved by all his comrades. He was most rigid in all that related to purity of morals, nor could he ever tolerate in conversation a word in the least opposed to Christian modesty, and he used to reprove severely, and even sometimes harshly anything that could offend it. His virtue was, however, exposed to a great danger. Without being in the least aware of it, he had been taken to a house of questionable repute; his lively manners inducing the hope of an easy triumph over his virtue ; but he came off victorious, full of indignation at the snare which had been laid for his innocence.

The same spirit of order and submission; the affection towards his superiors which had distinguished him during his studies in the college ; that same good spirit he had shown in every circumstance before, accompanied him in his military career. He always appeared happy and contented in the camp, whilst no soldier could be more faithful in the discharge of his military duties. He carried cleanliness almost to a fault, spending a considerable time in polishing his arms and brushing up his accoutrements. To see his radiant countenance in which, as in a mirror, was reflected his soul; his light graceful step; his jovial manner when on the march; to see all that and not to share his noble ardour was impossible.

" Why should we fear anything ?" he often said to his comrades. If your conscience be not at ease, why, there is our good confessor. Our cause is the very best of all, since we fight for God. We are immortal, what matter then the few days we sacrifice ? As for me, I have made an offering of my life to the Church and to Pius IX."

Through his irreproachable conduct, his piety, his amiable manners, he had won all hearts, and was without comparison the most popular man in the battalion. When one of his comrades uttered an unbecoming expression, he never failed to correct the offender, but he took care that his seasonable reproof should not appear one.

"Come now," he would say, "I am sure that word is not to be found in the dictionary of the Pope's soldiers." It was not enough for Guérin to edify his comrades by his good example, he also encouraged them by his words. No one possessed, as he did, the priceless gift of bearing up cheerfully against misfortunes; he perfectly understood the meaning of the proverb: "What we cannot cure, we must endure." So he never let any opportunity pass without availing himself of it to amuse his companions when they were tired or sad. But never did he appear to greater advantage than in the long and weary marches from Rome to the battlefield of Castelfidardo. It would have moved the coldest heart to admiration, to have seen him, short as he was, invariably marching in front, his musket on one shoulder, his knapsack on his back. Few among the volunteers being accustomed to such fatiguing journeys, had their feet litterally bleeding and felt quite exhausted; while others could not carry their arms or baggage, and worse still, had become dispirited and despondent. As for Guérin he never appeared in better spirits; he cheered all by his lively songs and animated anecdotes. He often took the rifle and knapsack from the weakest of the party, so that he was seen sometimes loaded with three instead of one. His equanimity of temper was unparalleled ; he was always himself. One day he lost his purse containing all the money he possessed, and to a friend who condoled with him on his misfortune, he simply said : "To be sure it is very unlucky, but that will not prevent me from fighting, for I have not lost my arms."

The little Pontifical army passed on the 17th of September near Loretto, whose venerated sanctuary they hailed with religious transports. The battle was expected for the following day. The gallant Commandant de Becdelieve concluded a magnificent address to the battalion in these beautiful words : " We are come here for the Pope's cause, which is God's own. Many among us will to-morrow by this time have been summoned to appear before the Almighty, and, as He requires. that our souls should be pure, let those who are afraid, that their consciences are not in perfect order, settle them at once. Our worthy chaplain here is ready to help them." Although Guérin had a few days ago been at confession, he was one of the first to comply with their truly Catholic Commanding Officer's admirable exhortation.

The battle was fought and lost. Guérin was among the wounded, having got a shot through his right lung. On a litter he was carried to a church at Castelfidardo, which was converted into a temporary hospital, and from there later removed to Osimo, where the Dominican monks took care of the wounded. The science of suffering is studied by few, while by still fewer it is reduced to practice. To endure the most acute bodily sufferings without a murmur, is the proof of a noble soul; but to bear with the same serenity of mind severe moral grief; to pardon those who add insult to persecution; to pray for the very authors of our death; to bear the heavy burden of suffering with an entire forgetfulness of self, coupled with an ardent love of God, is to ennoble suffering; and this is what Guérin uniformly did during the last days of protracted and excruciating agony. Guérin's patience in bearing the privation of necessaries, especially at first, when his bed was an old broken wooden box, on which he could hardly move, excited the admiration of all the attendants at the hospital. This great devotion prompted him to ask frequently for confession and communion. He encouraged his companions both by word and example to bear their sufferings with resignation and patience; in short, he was a model of edification to all who visited the hospital, and he was loved by every one who had the happiness of witnessing his angelic death, which occurred a few weeks afterwards.

CHAPTER VII.

§ 1.—The Soldier in Hospital.

Some General Remarks on Sickness.

If you were to contract a dangerous illness, what would you do, how take it? One man will say: "It cannot be helped, we must all die one day, and if it be my lot now, I must submit."

To another man death is very fearful. You must not speak of death to him; all through his illness you see plainly his great anxiety and fear.

The first of these two we term a fatalist, the second a coward. But the good Christian is neither a fatalist, nor a coward. He accepts sickness with resignation and conformity to the will of God. He knows that nothing happens in this world without the knowledge of God, or against His will, that He, our heavenly merciful Father chastises those whom He loves best. Such a conviction of mind and disposition of heart are unfailing sources of consolation. Besides, the sick man gains great merit by suffering patiently out of love, in union with; and after the example of, Jesus Christ and all the Saints, and in satisfaction for his sins, and is sustained by the hope of his reward and crown in heaven. The good Christian will ever suffer with patience. However great the pain, he will endure it all without murmuring. How hard it is to keep a man, without religious principles, from cursing and blaspheming everything. Nothing can please him.

The doctor, the medicine, the diet, the attendants are all inveighed against, and even Almighty God Himself is cursed by such a man. In fact, he is a burden, nay, a scandal to every one.

True patience is a hard enough virtue to practise under such trying circumstances, but God gives His grace to the sufferer who prays for it as he should, and a patient should therefore pray to God for it frequently, as it is the virtue he most requires now. After all, what is there in impatience? What good will or can come of it? Will it shorten our sufferings, or lessen them? The very reverse, of course. What so aggravates suffering as impatience,—what so alleviates it as patience?

Good health is a gift of God, but sickness is no less a gift. " A grievous sickness maketh the soul sober" (Ecc. XXXI. 2). Many Christians have become great saints in the course, and by the discipline, of a severe and protracted illness. Saint Lidwina is an instance. She lay sick for thirty-eight years, in constant great pain; during thirty years unable to leave her bed, and she suffered all with patience more wonderful than any of the miracles that she wrought about this time.

Often does the priest meet with patience truly heroic, during the course of his visits to patients in the hospitals and elsewhere. These patients die unknown to the world and in foreign countries; but their names are registered in the Book of Life.

§ 2.—Care of the Body.

The sick man has to take care of his body, I mean it is his duty so to do, as well as of his soul. Nobody may be indifferent or careless as regards the medical treatment he is under. The prescriptions of the doctor must be exactly observed. Soldiers, both in and out of hospital frequently do themselves great harm by not taking the prescribed medicine, making use, instead of medicines, of things utterly injurious to them.

The Christian should understand that it is his duty to respect his medical adviser, according to what the Holy Ghost says in Ecc. XXXVIII. v. 1. 2. & 4: " Honour the physician for the need thou hast of him; for the Most High hath created him; for all healing is from God. (v. 4). The Most High hath created medicines out of the earth, and a wise man will not abhor them."

Not that we may place all our confidence in the doctor alone. St. Basil writes: "We are to attribute not to the doctors, but to God alone, Who makes them operate as He pleases, the good or bad success of remedies." God sometimes restores health without any help from doctors or medicines; sometimes He works by means of them. At other times all consultations, all remedies, are useless; and it is He who bids them be so to teach us to place all our trust in Him alone. Therefore, always ascribe your recovery not so much to the doctor's care, as to God, Who alone has the power to cure all diseases. Wherefore it is written in the Book of Wisdom (XVI. 12): "It is not herbs nor fomentations, but O Lord, it is Thy word which has the virtue to heal all diseases."

And when it happens that the doctor does not understand your complaint, or has not taken that care which was required, you must attribute even this to the will of God. *

---

§. 3—Care of the Soul.

But of far greater importance than bodily health is the welfare of the soul. According to the Regulations of the Army, Military Chaplains are expected to visit the hospitals twice a week, or oftener, in order to impart religious consolation and instruction to the sick. The Catholic Priest has another object in view. His chief care is to save souls. The bodies are cared for by the doctors, apothecaries and others. Now, souls can only be saved and sinners converted by the Sacrament of Penance, and therefore the Catholic Priest takes advantage of the opportunity which sickness gives him of persuading the sick man to go to confession. The sick soldier is in bed and cannot escape. In a ward full of patients, indeed, like any one else under the influence of human respect, he shrinks, of course, from making his confession in the presence

---

* See Rodriguez' Christian Perfection.—Vol. 1.

of others. Nevertheless, a good confession can and must be made. Listen to this. Doctors, as a rule, conceal the gravity of the disease from the patient; the Priest cannot always—perhaps can seldom—tell whether the case is serious or not. The patient goes on unaware of his actual state, and in the sense of false security Confession is neglected, until the dreadful truth at last comes out, when, in many instances, it is unfortunately too late.

In the quiet orderly life in hospital the soldier will have time and freedom to read his prayers and examine his conscience. If he is ashamed to confess before his comrades, the Priest can generally choose his hour—when he is alone—or get a private room. But if the soldier is too ill to leave his bed, does he intend to lose his soul for fear of a comrade's sneer? And *will* his comrade sneer? No; soldiers though not good themselves ever respect those who are good, or who at least make an attempt to become good. Protestants, no less than Catholics, act in this manner.

Every soldier who goes into hospital, no matter how trifling his ailments may seem to be, should at once make his confession, that is, if he needs to do so—if in sin. An indisposition that seems to the patient and to the medical officer trivial at first may be the beginning of the last sickness.

How often does the last sickness come on in this way! Headache may be the symptom of approaching apoplexy. A feeling of debility and a slight fever may be the insidious signs of typhoid fever. A slight injury, a kick from a horse, and the like, may take an unhealthy turn. Pain, with an irritating fever is most likely to follow, and will undoubtedly preclude that calm attention which is so necessary to a good confession.

It is the opinion of all our medical officers that the progress of sickness in India is rapid, and it is asserted, on the best authority, that there is no greater obstacle to a cure being effected than a disturbed mind as there is no greater help towards a cure than a mind at rest. Peace of conscience puts the patient in the most favourable state for recovery. The sting of a bad conscience tends to bring about the very result the patient most fears.

Besides the incalculable advantage of the peace of heart which follows a good confession, there is the immediate removal from the occasions of sin which he enjoys in hospital. A man who has been the slave of vice should seize the rare opportunity of renouncing it, whilst in hospital, altogether. He is removed from all temptation which his bad habits render it so difficult to resist, to overcome the vice. Seize the time thus offered, when vice cannot be indulged in.

Many a man who from his weakness would never have reformed, if surrounded with the temptations of life outside, has left hospital an altered man.

Every vice is strengthened by indulgence in it; in hospital that indulgence is difficult to procure, and is easy to abstain from; but the man who would indulge in his vice there would only teaze and worry himself—the means of gratification are not there. God, Who knows your weakness and your difficulties sends you sickness in order that you may make use of it; that it may help towards your reformation.

Looked upon as the only, or at least the indispensable, means of amending a bad life and avoiding a bad death; or looked upon as putting one in the most favourable condition for the recovery of bodily health—whether you think of the soul or the body—in whatever light you may regard confession, it should be made as soon as possible after entering the hospital.

§ 4.—How to spend Leisure Hours.

This is a question of the greatest importance, especially if a man is confined for many weeks or months to bed. He may be too ill to read—reading may be very bad for him. But so far as he can, without any risk, it is just the time to read. If he is not too ill, he should read; but not the newspapers and novels supplied from the Garrison Library. He may read something more useful, anything innocent, though amply amusing. After being reconciled to God, he is supposed to have a greater relish for religious books; they console, they instruct, they counsel him to a good life. The Chaplain will be only too glad to lend him books of this kind, which do marvellously strengthen good resolutions, and show the way to imitate Christ and His Saints. Saint Ignatius is only one—truly an illustrious one—of ten thousand instances of this, that is, of the fruit you may expect from reading when seriously sick. In Alban Butler's "Lives of the Saints" you will find the memorable instance mentioned concerning a soldier's conversion by reading good books in time of illness. In 1521 there was war between France and Spain. The French were besieging Pampeluna; it was defended by Ignatius, then a very young officer in the Spanish army. The garrison had resolved to surrender, in spite of all Ignatius could do, and the gates were already open to the enemy when Ignatius retired to the citadel. There, at the head of the little handful of men who followed him he endeavoured to hold the place and drive back the enemy, but in the heat of the fight a cannon ball struck both his legs, severely bruising one, and breaking the other. He fell, and the garrison, seeing his fall, surrendered at discretion. The French treated the prisoners well, especially Ignatius in consideration of his bravery. They carried him to the General's quarters, and soon after removed him to his own castle, Loyola. During his illness, whilst the surgeons had to set his legs, he found the time tedious, and called for something to read. He thought only of romances,—he had always been fond of such reading. No such books strange to say, were then to be found in the Castle of Loyola, and, stranger still, there was found a volume of the Life of our Saviour, and the Lives of the Saints. This was brought to him. He read it at first only to pass the time, but afterwards began to relish it, and to pass all days in reading it. He chiefly admired in the Saints their love of solitude and of the Cross. He considered, among the hermits how many people of quality, there were who had buried themselves in caves and dens, pale with fasting, and covered with hair-cloth, and he said to himself:—"These men were of the same frame as I am of; why then should I not do as they have done?" He made his resolution to become a saint, and immediately after his recovery he went to a chapel, hung up his sword at the altar of the Blessed Virgin and consecrated himself to the service of God alone. Now this officer is the same great Ignatius of Loyola who founded the Society of Jesus, and who is renowned in the History of the Catholic Church for the wonderful things done by him and by the Society he founded for the glory of God and the salvation of souls.

§. 5.—The Chaplain's Visit.

The sick soldier should always be glad to see the Priest. Many shrink from his visits, avoid him if they can, and this for different reasons. It often happens that neither the Catholic Priest nor the Protestant Minister can find out who belongs to their flock.

A card hangs above each patient's cot for the guidance of the visiting Chaplains. On one side is printed " Church of England," on the reverse, " Roman Catholic." Some men, on observing the approach of their Chaplains reverse their card, others hide them altogether, while others again will exchange cards with their neighbours. In a certain place on one occasion at all events the Minister on visiting the hospital found all the patients in one ward marked with the designation of " Roman Catholic," though there was really not one Roman Catholic in it; and, alas! Catholics in that place used to play the same trick, and get " Church of England" or " Church of Scotland" cards, to make the Priest believe that they were not of his persuasion. When a bad Catholic has no time to escape the visiting Priest, an easier trick is to feign sleep which can be done at once, as soon as the Priest is seen—and of course he is safe in that case. Those who are allowed to walk about hide themselves in the wash house, or in some other ward; and it is a real fact, that men have been for months in hospital, and have never been spoken to by their clergymen— they have never been able to get at them. Looking at such conduct from a mere worldly point of view, it must be called anything but noble, or even manly or civil; but marvellously ungrateful, rude, and childish. Why should a gentleman kindly visiting any one be treated in this manner? For a Catholic soldier the consequences may be very serious. How often does it happen that the Priest knows nothing whatever of his illness, and is only called when it is too late!

---

§. 6.—The Last Rites of the Church.

When once your illness becomes serious, and there is danger, you are bound to receive the last Sacraments, viz.—Holy Communion and Extreme Unction. There is a special obligation to receive Communion in such a case. It strengthens you against temptation, (and then, if ever, you need being strengthened); so a Christian would be guilty of a mortal sin, did he, on his death-bed, refuse to communicate.

In Catholic countries the taking of the Blessed Sacrament to the sick is a most solemn ceremony. The church bell is rung, and people assemble with candles in procession to accompany the Blessed Sacrament to the house of the sick. Generally there is a Confraternity, whose principal business is thus to assist the dying, thus to honour the Blessed Sacrament. The priest carries the Blessed Sacrament publicly through the streets, with his head uncovered, whilst four men hold the canopy over him. It is a pity that, in military hospitals, not only all show must be avoided, but also certain circumstances render it difficult to administer the Viaticum with even only becoming decency and reverence.

But some kind of preparation should be always made by getting the little table which is near each patient's bed cleared and covered with a napkin or towel so that the priest may place on it all the articles he requires for the occasion. Where there is a Catholic apothecary or matron such a preparation is easily made. It often happens that several Catholic soldiers are in the same ward. If they are not confined to their beds, they should assist with devotion at the ceremony, and not behave in that indifferent, disrespectful manner, which only ignorance and unbelief can excuse. Wherefore, do not walk out; do not smoke your pipes in the verandah; do not talk whilst the Eucharistic God is in your presence. No, no,—do not make that sacrifice of your faith to human respect, and to the irreligion by which you are surrounded.

The orderly, the man who is placed in charge of the patient, can do much good and earn much hereafter, by doing his duty to the best of his ability. However, he should not look after the bodily comfort of the patient alone, there are his spiritual wants also to be attended to. Why not say a few words to him that affords religious consolation? A few simple words might be so useful, so consoling! Why not read to him a few lines from a Prayer-Book, or some other religious book? This would be a great act of charity in the comrade who visits the sick man on the days appointed. Many instances have occurred of souls being saved by the kind influence of visitors, the patients being apparently influenced by them, even after the clergyman had failed to convert them; also of patients making timely confession and receiving the last Sacraments without which they would have died, but for such a true friend having conveyed to the priest information as to the dangerous state they were in.

When there is danger the sick man should also receive the Sacrament of *Extreme Unction*—that great Sacrament in which the sick are anointed with holy oil, and through the priest's prayer receive the grace of God for the good of their souls always, and often times for the health of their bodies. Protestants do not believe in this Sacrament; strange is this disbelief! Should one of them ask you, on what authority the priest anoints the sick? simply ask him, or her, to show you the Bible. Open it, and find the 5th Chapter of the Epistle of St. James, and show him the 14th and 15th verses, and ponder thereon with gratitude yourself: " Is any man sick among you, let him bring in the priests of the Church, and let them pray over him, anointing him with oil in the name of the Lord, and the prayer of faith shall save the sick man, and the Lord shall raise him up, and if he have committed sins they shall be forgiven him."

There are, we may be sure, three enemies, who assault the soul of the dying man before he departs this life. Death with its horrors and pains; conscience with its remorse; the devil with his temptations. Even when we enjoy good health the thought of death saddens us, but what will it be when it is close at hand and the agony of death has begun? Then conscience also properly wakes up and all the sins we have committed come before us. The devil, too, is busy in tempting the soul, or rather puts forth all his power—does all he can—to secure it. Where shall the soul find strength to fight against the world, the flesh, and the devil!

Behold, the priest of God comes! "Peace be to this house," he says. He has the holy oil with him, to administer to you a Sacrament instituted by Christ, for this very time—this last combat—to give corporal and spiritual comfort to the sick. It is the last anointing which the Catholic receives. In Baptism he was anointed on his breast, and shoulders, and head for first time; in Confirmation the Bishop anointed his brow with the chrism of salvation; on his death-bed he is anointed for the last time on the eyes, ears, nostrils, lips, hands and feet—the organs of the five senses. Now, whilst the priest applies this holy oil to his eyes, his ears, and other senses, the sick man should, with a contrite and humble heart implore the mercy of God to forgive all the sins, which through these different avenues have made their way into his soul. How great are the graces and benefits promised by God to all who receive this Sacrament with the proper disposition! He will save the sick man, and raise him up from the sick bed, if he sees his recovery expedient for the good of his soul; and what is infinitely more desirable than the health of the body, he will impart to him the forgiveness of his sins.

There is probably not one priest who has had for any time to administer Extreme Unction and who has not seen the, so to say, miraculous effects of this Sacrament. In 1877 when the cholera was raging in the city and camp of Ahmednagar, one Saturday night, after 11 o'clock, the Priest was sent for to attend a patient, a Private of the 66th Regiment, who had been given up by the Doctor. He was in a state of collapse, which is the fore-runner of death. "Now make your confession," said the priest, "and I shall anoint you, if you wish." "Yes Father," replied the dying man with his feeble voice, "I am a member of the Confraternity, do you not know me? I go to Holy Communion, as the rule enjoins on the first Sunday of every month, and now I am glad and happy for I am well prepared." After having made his short confession he was anointed, but could not receive holy Communion on account of the vomiting which still continued. It was only half an hour later, when the Doctor made inquiry as to whether the man was dead. "No;" said the Apothecary, "he seems to have got over the crisis." And so it was. Shortly after having received Extreme Unction he was out of danger. A fortnight afterwards the man was again fit for duty. He lived until the 27th July 1880, on which day he died a soldier's death on the battle-field of Maiwand, in Afghanistan.

How blessed a thing to be always prepared for death! But of all the difficulties which prevent a good confession, none is so great as the difficulty of speech, or want of consciousness. Happy the man who has settled the affairs of his soul in good time!

Whilst the 11th Regiment was stationed at Poona in 1878, cholera broke out and carried away many victims. One Saturday evening an old soldier came to St. Patrick's Chapel, wishing particularly to see the Priest. "I come to make my confession," said he, "and I have got a young chap with me who has not been to confession for the last seven years. I got him to come along with me for a walk, and brought him up to this Chapel. 'Now,' says I, 'let us say a handful of prayers inside for the good of our souls,' and he came in with me. 'I am going to confession,' says I to him, 'you had better come too.' But he would not. At last he gave me his consent, and he is now inside preparing for his confession." Both were reconciled with God, and received Holy Communion on Sunday morning at the Soldiers' Mass. About a fortnight afterwards the same Priest got a sick call,— it was to a cholera patient. He was very ill indeed and had lost the power of speech. "What a pity," thought the Priest, "that I was not called sooner. The man will not be able to make his confession; and all I can do will be to give him conditional absolution and anoint him." But as soon as he saw the poor dying man, he thought he had seen him before, and that but recently. Yes, it was the young soldier who had thrown off his load of sin on that Saturday evening, and who had ever since been leading a very exemplary life. He received the last consolations of the Church with apparent devotion, and soon afterwards died a happy death.

Here now follows another incident which will greatly edify you. It is a real fact, and a miracle of the mercy of God.

§ 7.—An incident of Indian Life. *

Father Francisco, the Portuguese Chaplain to the troops stationed at Gurrumpore in Upper Bengal, was sitting in his bungalow one day in the hot season of 1860, endeavouring as well as the intense heat would permit to prosecute his Hindostanee studies. The hot winds were blowing outside with great fierceness, but the Chaplain was too poor to turn them to account by employing a native to throw water on the kuskus mats that blocked up the whole length of the verandah, and thus produce a cooling evaporation, and for the same reason the huge punkah that was slung

---
*Lamp, 1867.

from the roof remained motionless, and distributed no reviving draughts of air through the close atmosphere of the large darkened room.

Presently the mid-day gun boomed from the front of the soldier's lines, and as the good Priest rose after saying the Angelus a loud cry of " Boy ! boy !" from the compound announced the approach of a visitor, and Sooka, Father Francisco's only servant, entered with the information that a soldier sahib want to see masta."

" Very well, Sooka ; show him in ;" and a tall fine looking soldier, his eyes dazed by the strong glare of the outside sun, stumbled through the windowless room, saluted, and asked in a timid voice if he could have a few moments' conversation.

Certainly ; I am delighted to see you, Dilvin ; just sit down there, said the Priest as he pushed a chair towards his visitor, whom he recognised as one of the blackest sheep of his flock, and a man whose heart he had been quite unable to touch in matters of religion.

"Something has come over me, Sir," began Dilvin, in a low voice; "I don't well know what, but I thought I'd step over and just ask, if you thought there was any chance of such a man as me ever becoming a good Catholic ; and I've been a bad man, Sir—a very bad man all my life, and never minded religion since I was a boy, Sir; and now I'm afraid it is too late—but still I thought I'd tell you—

"It is never too late to repent in this life, Dilvin," said Father Francisco in a soothing voice, "and you well know that our good Saviour came to call sinners and not the just to repentance."

"I know, Sir, I know; but I have been so very bad (this with a deep sigh), I can hardly think my repenting would be any good, because—in fact, it is fear with me, and not religion."

The fear of God is the beginning of wisdom; and then the Priest talked in a low comforting tone of the wonderful mercy of our good God; of His great desire for sinners to come to Him; of the efficacy of the Sacrament of Penance, and of the power of grace for reconciliation with an offended Creator; and when he saw that his words had taken effect, and that the rough powerful man before him, who had always seemed alike fearless of God and man, was actually sobbing like a child, he asked him to kneel down with him, and offered up a fervent prayer, that God would continue to shower down His grace until the blessed gift of perfect repentance was attained.

The soldier was much affected, and on rising sketched with great humility the chief events of a wild and sinful career, with a view to obtaining such instruction as might be necessary before preparing for a general confession.

Robert Dilvin had been educated at a good middle-class Catholic school, from which at the age of sixteen he had run away to sea, and then on the breaking out of the Crimean war had enlisted as a soldier, and gone through the whole of the miseries, hardships, and dangers of that campaign, without having once experienced the slightest fear either for soul or body. He had plunged into every vice and riot that came within his reach, and although a smart and first rate soldier on parade, was well known as one of the most incorrigible scamps in the regiment.

During the Indian mutiny he had shown the most dauntless bravery, and would have been promoted over and over again, had it not been for his evil reputation. In all these years he had utterly ignored religion, and though of course obliged to parade for Mass on Sundays had proved quite deaf to all religious exhortations and remonstrances and had lived as if there was no God. One thing he had done, but as he confessed himself, it was more from human affection than with any pious motive—he had always worn the little medal of the Immaculate Conception which his poor mother had placed round his neck on her death-bed, and had at times, often at long intervals, said a Hail Mary with a sort of half intention of begging the Blessed Virgin's intercession that he might some day repent.

For ten long weary years he had been a stranger to the Sacraments, and now, as he bade adieu for the present to the good Priest, he repeated that it seemed to be fear that was driving him to seek a reconciliation with God, and not a true disposition to repentance.

"But what do you fear, Dilvin?" asked Father Francisco, as he walked towards the door to show his guest out.

"Death, Sir; I never felt it before; but now every time there is a cholera case, or I hear the band playing the Dead March in Saul as we file down to bury some poor fellow, I get quite nervous, and am an utter coward."

Father Francisco laughed gently, and said he wished a few more would fear death in that manner and then, making an appointment for the day after next, to get up the scaffolding, as it were, for a general confession, shook Dilvin warmly by the hand and dismissed him.

On the two following mornings Dilvin was one of the few worshippers at the early Mass; but when three o'clock came on the appointed day and he did not appear at the Priest's bungalow, the latter began to fear that the enemy had been too powerful, and that a change had taken place in the soldier's sentiments. In about an hour's time he had ceased thinking on the subject, and was on his way to the lines to visit a poor sick soldier's wife, when he met a man who was bringing him a message to say that Dilvin had been seized with cholera, and was now in hospital, and, during the intervals of the paroxysms of pain, was asking anxiously for Father Francisco.

Immediately the Priest hurried off, and found the poor fellow writhing in all the awful pains of this most fearful disease. The two Assistant Surgeons of the regiment were standing by the side of the charpoy on which the sufferer lay, and applying every possible remedy they could think of to procure him relief; but nought seemed to be of any avail, and it was evident they both thought the case desperate.

"Too late Sir, Oh, too late!" groaned out the patient, as the Priest hastily took his place at the head of the cot, "too late—I'am lost—justly—only what I deserve—deathbed repentance can be no good;—and after such a life as mine—Oh!" and he screamed aloud in his agony. Then the good Priest knelt down by the bedside and spoke sweet words of mercy and love and hope—dismissing the attendants from the immediate neighbourhood—exhorted and pressed the sin-laden sufferer to make such confession as he could, and to trust in the infinite mercy of God, who can forgive more than we can offend, pointing out that the intention of repentance and amendment and even a sort of preliminary confession, had been in existence before the dire malady had set in, and that therefore this could hardly be deemed a case of death-bed repentance. And so the strange scene went on in the increasing darkness—for the burning sun had now gone down, and the cool evening breeze played fitfully in through the open doors and wide verandah—and by the light of a single oil lamp that drew a dismal, yellow, indistinct glare over every object, and between the spasms of the greatest agony the human frame can experience, the prostrate man told in broken sentences the awful tale of a life of sins. All the sad catalogue of human weakness, folly, and passion; all the foul stains that had defiled that once pure and innocent soul; all the crimes that the wild storms of a rebellious flesh, devil-excited, had driven his unhappy soul into committing; all the daily and hourly contempt of God, of which the life of an irreligious man is made up; all the sad volume of possible sin which Satan has compiled for the ruin of mankind;—all—all were poured out with heart-rending gasps of bodily and mental agony; while ever and anon the melancholy wail of the troops of jackals that scoured across the adjoining sandy plain in search of carrion broke in as a ghastly chorus. Now and again the surgeons approached to see if any change showed itself of which advantage might be taken, but none such appeared, and presently they retired altogether, having decided that in a very short time collapse must set in, and then—death!

There was no time to be lost; and, the confession having been ended, Father Francisco hastened to speak the blessed words of absolution. One glance of unutterable gratitude came over the handsome features of the soldier—a shudder, a sort of shrinking into himself, and then he became insensible.

The Priest thought he was dead, but it was not so; and he sat by the bedside praying fervently for mercy for the parting spirit. The noiseless Hindoo Hospital Assistants, in whom hope never dies, piled blankets and rugs over the inanimate form, and then squatted quietly on their haunches round the cot and smoked their hubble-bubbles as they crooned drearily one to another, and waited for the coming of life or death. perfectly indifferent which it might be, and yet prepared to take advantage of any favourable change.

" Well, Padre! by Jove you 're a better doctor than any of us! you ought to take out a degree and set up as a sawbones," said Dr. Martin, as he met Father Francisco taking his morning walk some few days after the above events.

" Perhaps I will, Doctor, when you retire and give up your practice to me. But how do you find Dilvin this morning?"

" O getting on famously, and picking up strength at an immense rate. By Jupiter, he had a narrow shave of it; I would'nt have given a cowrie for his chance when I left him that night. But now he is as right as nine pence. Ta, ta!" And the young Surgeon stuck spurs into his tatoo and galloped home to his breakfast.

And so in truth it was; Dilvin, instead of getting into a state of collapse and dying, had in a few hours broken out into a profuse perspiration, and gradually mended, until he actually was now, as Dr. Martin said, getting on famously. In about ten days he was convalescent, and in due course left the hospital, apparently not much the worse for his close combat with the grim King of Terrors.

When Dilvin resumed his duty he was a changed man, and thenceforth led a most blameless and correct life, and was evidently endeavouring by good example to atone, in some measure, for the evil his bad conduct had caused to his comrades. No man in the regiment was more assiduous in his attendance at the services of the little chapel and no man evinced so plainly the saving mercy of God's grace, as shown in the meek, humble and contrite manner in which he now conducted himself as the former scapegrace Robert Dilvin. His conversion seemed to want in nothing; and Father Fransisco had good reason to be proud of his convert, and to hope that there was indeed joy in heaven for the repentance of so public and notorious a sinner. And when the remaining portion of the hot season had passed, and the rains came, and they also in turn passed, and the glaring burning sun once more appeared, and by its powerful rays drew from the saturated earth the deadly and noxious steams of rotting vegetation, then came the trying time; and miasma, fever, and the life-destroying jungle fever ruled triumphant in Gurrumpore, and drew into the silent grave many and many a poor victim who had not the requisite stamina to resist their dread embrace.

In this time of death the undaunted bravery and true religion of Dilvin shone conspicuous, and he never seemed to rest or take his ease while he could be of any use to the numerous fever-stricken men who crowded the hospital to excess.

He read, he prayed, he exhorted; he held up his own former shameful life in comparison with his present happiness before the eyes of his suffering comrades, in hopes of turning their eyes also to the wonderful mercy of God, and Father Francisco over and over again declared that this recently-converted man did more good in bringing sinners to God than all his own exertions and entreaties. His one word was "mercy"—the mercy God had shown to him, and the mercy He would show to all who desired to come to Him. He spoke of mercy to the strong in the barrack bungalow, or on guard; he read of mercy to the weak and ailing in the hospital, and he whispered mercy in the ear of the dying. But it was the last, Our Redeemer had marked him for His own, and ordained not to leave him in this weary world.

A headache, a desperate sense of weakness, a weariness and desire of sleep-rest, a faintness, a shivering, and Robert Dilvin was soon wrapped up in blankets and carried off to hospital never to leave it alive. His end was one of peace; and after receiving all the glorious aids of our Holy Church, he calmly died; and the last word the weeping Priest heard from his lips was "Mercy."

In the well-filled graveyard at Gurrumpore there is a humble stone erected by sorrowing comrades to his memory. The name, the date of death, the age, are duly inscribed in fair characters, and underneath by way of epitaph is the single, blessed word "Mercy."

CHAPTER VIII.

§ 1.—The Soldier in trouble.

Causes of getting into trouble.

Besides the hospital, there is another place which a military Chaplain has to visit, namely, the prison. For minor offences the British soldier is usually only detained in cells; but if tried by a District or General Court-Martial, and sentenced to a long period of imprisonment, he will be sent to a central military prison, of which there is one in each Presidency. And why is the man in prison?—how does he get there? Statistics make strange revelations. Every visiting Chaplain finds out that insubordination is the crime that has brought most men into trouble,— insubordination of which *drink* has been the cause,— drink which has led him into bad company to gamble; that means by which a man's bad passions are aroused. He has sold his kit or stolen, or, it may be, he has committed some more trifling crime in itself. But in all such cases, had the man only had a stronger control over his passions; if he had borne in mind that submission and obedience are the first duties of a soldier, he would not have got into such great trouble.

Subordination of one creature to another that has a higher rank is a part of that great order of things made by Almighty God Himself. There could be no harmony, no order, in this world (there would be nothing but confusion and disorder in it) had not God established certain laws and rules by which the world is governed. From the Bible we learn that God has made everything in this order of subordination. "Thou hast ordered all things in *measure* and *number* and *weight*" (Wisdom XI, 21.) Chemistry, Natural History in all its parts, and Astronomy, the more we know of these sciences, bear their witness to the same truth, and show that the inferior elements are everywhere ruled by superior powers, and thus is the perfect order in the world effected. They confirm this text of Scripture. The heavens themselves move around one centre. Moons move around their planets, and the planets around their suns, and the stars still follow the same courses which were assigned to them on the day of their creation. Innumerable angels surround the throne of the Almighty, but even among them there is subordination; for, as we gather from different texts of the Bible, they are divided into nine hierarchies. In like manner men must obey others who are their superiors. Such is the will of God. All superiors have their power from God, or as St. Paul (Romans XIII.) writes: "There is no Power except from God, and he who resists Power resists God." "Servants," says the same Apostle in his Epistle to the Ephesians, Chapter VI, v. 5, "obey your masters with fear and trembling, in the simplicity of your hearts, as Christ: not serving to the eye, as it were pleasing men, but as the servants of

Christ, doing the will of God from the heart." To this we may add: "Soldiers, obey your superior officers! Though they may be sinners, unbelievers, or heathens, they have their power from God, and must be obeyed in every point where there is no sin." How obedient were the Christian soldiers who served in the Roman legions under pagan emperors! They made no difficulty about drawing the sword against the enemies of their country; but when anything was required of them, which religion condemned, they firmly refused to obey, and chose, (although in sufficient force to defend themselves), rather to be slaughtered than displease God.

Obedience, as you know, is one of the vows taken in Religious Orders, and obedience there is by far more difficult than military obedience in the Service. Monks and Nuns must not only go wherever they are sent to, and do whatever their superiors may order them to do, they must conform their will and judgment to the will and judgment of a superior; they must receive all orders as from God Himself, and execute them with attention, exactness, and cheerfulness. St. Ignatius enjoins on his disciples the strictest obedience, and urges them to excel in this virtue,—to be as thoroughly without opposition as a corpse is supple; and manageable as is a staff which an old man uses for any purpose he may want it. Oh! what merits for heaven could not a Christian soldier gain, did he obey all the orders of his superior officers in a true Christian spirit. His duties are indeed works which he is first of all often obliged to perform—those things he so little values,—those things in themselves, of so little worth. There only needs the good intention, and these most ordinary actions are surely sanctified. Say every morning something to this effect : " All I have to do this day shall be done out of love of God, for the glory of God." You will derive immense benefit from that good intention, it will influence and give its spirit to everything you do that day. Many soldiers believe that there is nothing wrong in breaking a rule or an order, so long as they are not found out. Many things against order are done, and many irregularities are committed without notice being taken of them. The sentry on guard, the orderly man in the Barrack room, the sick in hospital, often break their rules and think that there is no harm in doing so, as long as no report is made. But there is at all events, this harm in it, it is all against the spirit and obligations of religion and conscience. More than this they expose themselves to the greatest danger of coming to grief. True, it is possible that there is no sin in doing acts against an order simply penal, that is given under the pain of punishment; however, a good Catholic will be very careful and abstain from such acts. He will obey the most trifling orders and regulations after the example of Jesus Christ, who, though so great, was subject to Mary and Joseph at Nazareth for so many years in everything, and at last was obedient unto death, even the death of the cross. Commanding Officers know how to appreciate such conscientious men, and do not hesitate to entrust to them the most responsible positions.

§ 2.—Behaviour whilst in Prison.

Now, if you have been so unfortunate as to have committed a military crime for which you have been tried by a Court-Martial, and perhaps sentenced to imprisonment for a long period, let us see how you can make the best of it, and how you should behave in prison.

(1). Make a firm resolution to keep all the Prison Rules. They are strict indeed, and you may often break this rule or that without any notice being taken of it and may escape, but it is a dangerous thing, and also wrong. You miss your tobacco, and there will be many an opportunity of getting a smoke. But it is against the regulation, and extra punishment will be awarded to you if you are discovered and reported. Therefore keep on the safe side.

(2). Do everything you are ordered with the readiness and cheerfulness you would if you were paid for it. So your behaviour will be appreciated by the Prison authorities, and you will be allowed many little privileges which are withheld from the refractory and unmanageable. To this behaviour you have only to add the higher motive of Christianity and from good sense it rises to a Christian virtue.

(3.) Bear your imprisonment with patience. Just call to mind what so many Martyrs and Saints have had to endure, and that they were innocent and holy and suffered for Christ; while you are far from being innocent. Still you can also suffer for Christ, if you wish, for all the sins of your past life, patiently, and in resignation to the will of God.

(4.) Follow and take to heart the advice and the consolation which the Priest visiting the prison will be so glad to give. What abundant opportunity, time and quiet, you have here for making your Confession as often as you please and preparing for Holy Communion once a month or oftener, and when the influence of human respect is reduced to the lowest degree, for there are, so to say, none in prison to pass their remarks on you, none thus to hinder you from complying with all your religious duties.

(5). Like the man in hospital, you should spend your lonely leisure hours in reading. None but religious books, or at least instructive, and therefore, in their way, edifying, are allowed to prisoners, and therefore you need not be warned against reading bad books. If there be no Prison Library, you can obtain books from the visiting Priest. But, in accepting Protestant books, be careful,—I would say, do not touch them, unless they do not contain religious doctrine. There are no end of tracts served out by the Minister and Scripture Reader. Do not accept of any, nor read them, no, not even to pass the time. Among those Catholic religious books you should read above all explanations of the Christian doctrine, the Bible History, the sufferings of Our Lord, the lives of Martyrs and other Saints. Have you never seen the "Imitation or the Following of Christ?" It is a beautiful little book, in which you may read a chapter every day, and then reflect on what you have read, for it affords great satisfaction. You may also probably improve yourself in some branch of learning, as History, Geography, Arithmetic, &c.

(6.) Whilst in prison, you have also plenty of time to say your prayers regularly, morning and evening, before and after meals, and when the bell rings for the "Angelus." It is a good practice to say the Rosary every day; and if you are without beads say it on your ten fingers.

(7.) There is another point to which you must pay great attention. In every prison you will find men who are regular old gaol-birds, and who are up to every trick and mischief. They often, in spite of all the rules, find means of leading the young and inexperienced astray, and get them by their wicked advice into further trouble, whilst they themselves manage to evade it. Such was the case with a young Artillery man in the Poona Prison a couple of years ago. He had to do three years there, and the very first month he managed to get into hot water. A sort of conspiracy was going on, and, when discovered, these old gaol-birds threw all the blame on him. He was sentenced to be flogged (50 lashes), whilst the real malefactors, the instigators of the plot, got off scot free.

§ 3— On being released from Prison.

The nearer the time of your release approaches, the more careful you should be to keep out of trouble. Think over what you will do when out of prison. Make good and firm resolutions for the future. You have had a good opportunity of learning a good lesson, which you should not forget as long as you live. If drink was the cause of your misfortune, resolve to take the pledge for the time you have to serve in the Army. You may take it before leaving the prison. If gambling and bad company have brought you to this trouble you must keep away from such false friends as you have been friendly with before. Many men, after being released from prison, have distinguished themselves by their good religious life, and have regained the good character which they had lost by their wildness and folly. But many, nay *most*, soon get into trouble again, because they commence drinking and committing the same crimes as before and at last come to lose all their years of service, and after years of imprisonment are discharged with ignominy from the service. Then what remains to them but a miserable life as loafers or beggars, and death at last in some workhouse at home. Take a warning from such examples, and you will become happy and content enough even whilst you are in the Service, and after your discharge from it you will be able to gain for yourself an honest livelihood, and die a good Christian in your own country, perhaps in the very place where you were born and brought up, and where your forefathers are sleeping and awaiting the day of a glorious resurrection.

CHAPTER IX.

The Soldiers Self-Improvement.

In this Chapter you will read something about the good use you can make of your leisure-hours, and the advantages offered to you from a worldly point of view.

"Why stand you here all the day idle?" Thus said the landlord in the Parable to those men whom he found standing in the market place doing nothing. They were poor people,—labourers who had to work for their livelihood; but on that day they had no employment, for they replied, "Because nobody has engaged us." But what would the landlord have said if they had been idlers in the proper sense of the word? Certainly they would have deserved a sharp reprimand. Idleness is one of the greatest dangers a soldier has to avoid, especially in India. During the heat of the day he cannot leave barracks. After morning parade he has nothing to do, particularly in an Infantry corps. So the men are lying on their cots; some spend their time in reading foolish books and paperss, some are smoking their pipes all the day long chatting here and their to no purpose. They only kill time by doing nothing. And in the evening they loiter about the Canteen, the Coffee shop, and the Bazaar until the gun fires and calls them back to barracks. In this manner years are spent without any profit, and when their time is expired they go home as ignorant as they were on the day of their enlistment. They may have a few pounds in the bank to start with in civil life, but they have learnt nothing but soldiering and can do nothing but what they did before they enlisted.

In time of peace every soldier in India has much time at his disposal, and many leisure hours after regimental duties are over. The Military Authorities combining with the Government of India do their best to give the men opportunities for their self-improvement, and it is the sodier's own fault if he does not mak use of them.

§. 1.—First there are—

The Workshops.

These are places where soldiers may learn a trade; or, when they know one already, they may obtain useful and also profitable employment. The shops are always close to the barracks, and therefore within easy reach of the regimental workmen. Where practicable, a separate apartment is provided for these shops : the armourers, the tailors, the printers, the bookbinders, the bakers. These various shops are superintended by an officer, who looks after their interior economy, regulates the hours of work, and gives rewards to these soldier mechanics, who are useful in time of peace as they are in time of war, the whole of these arrangements being subject to the Officer Commanding.

If a soldier accepts the advantages offered to him by joining a workshop, he will soon find how the monotony of Indian life is checked by mechanical labour; and when his time of service is up, he will look back with pleasure to the hours he spent so greatly to his advantage in the regimental workshops. The married man especially will be benefited by it; his children will learn from him habits of industry and will afterwards put into practice what they have witnessed in their earlier days. As the parents, so also the children will be. Great encouragement is given to the soldier-mechanic every year on the occasion of the Industrial Exhibition. Indeed, when visiting such an Exhibition one is astonished at the taste and perfection shown in the manufacture of the various articles then offered for sale. The prizes which the soldiers receive in addition are very liberal and are calculated to stimulate the men to exert all their knowledge and skill.

Lastly, when the British soldier goes home, he will be useful to himself, to his family, to his neighbours, provided, I say, he has taken advantage of the opportunities offered to him when he was in the service. He then perhaps may make himself that useful personage we call "a Jack of all trades."

There was, in the first Battalion of the 2nd Queen's Regiment an old Irishman, who had spent more than twenty years in India. He was no scholar, as it is called, nor a tradesman by profession. He was only a *fly-catcher*. When the season came he was always out with his net and bag after butterflies and moths. These he fixed on needles, neatly arranged under a glass case, and sent them to the Industrial Exhibition. His arrangements were very tasteful, and besides the prize he got from the Committee, he cleared about a hundred rupees by the sale of his work. And as he went on repeating the same thing for years, in the end he put nearly a hundred pounds into the regimental bank, a sum which came very handy to him when he returned to Europe. There are many different kinds of industrious work done by soldiers during their leisure-hours; surely none of these men were sorry for having thus spent their time; only the idler, the lazy man who lounges about the barracks all day long with his black pipe in his mouth forfeits these advantages.

Old soldiers have often derived the greatest benefit from working in the shops. I knew a man, an old gunner of the late 6th Brigade R. A., who left the station at Colaba with over Rs. 2,000 to his credit in the Regimental Savings' Bank, every piece of which was earned in the workshop, and this with a wife and three children to support. Now, this man was no tradesman in the technical sense of the word, merely a *handy man*, who had learned how to make tables, boxes, and the like. Could he have done this in civil life?

Many old soldiers, who have not learnt to utilise the workshops, are, as a rule, discontented, unhappy men, having no resources beyond drinking, smoking, and gambling, to pass even an hour pleasantly. They may often be seen in the morning near the back doors of Sergeants' Messes looking for a superstitious peg or pint, and when not in hospital, are almost invariably employed on work in the corps they belong to, which would be considered objectionable by superior men, e. g., such as looking after conservancy business. A man of that stamp cannot, when he leaves the service, settle down in a comfortable home. He can only swell by one more the number of wretched human beings, already, alas! too large, or take his place in some poor-house for a short time before a pauper's grave receives him. Had he taken advantage of learning something in the regimental workshop, his future would have been quite different. Although a pensioner can only live in a humble way, yet when he has acquired habits of thrift and industry he will be able to pass away a pleasant and useful life. At all events he is above immediate want.

However, it must also be remarked, that the soldier mechanic, like every other employed man in the regiment who makes some extra money, must be temperate and not spend in drink what he earns by his work. It is a fact that many men work in the shops only in order to get more money for drink. Thus they always get into trouble and come to greater grief than they would if they had not worked. As a rule, the more money a soldier gets the more he spends in drink. Where is a sober shoeing-smith? or a temperate rough-rider who gets a good deal of extra pay for breaking-in horses? In a Battery of Artillery no body can make more money than they. Cabinet-makers who work for officers and gentlemen in the station, collar-makers, armourer sergeants, photographers, hospital writers, and many others can make a good deal of money but generally speaking, very little of it is put into the bank. It is a pity to see men who are so clever at their trade always getting into trouble.

There was in 1877 a soldier of the 66th Regiment at Ahmednagar, an excellent carpenter. The articles he sent to the Poona Exhibition were the best of their kind, and for them he got good prizes and distinctions. But he spent in a very short time all his money in drink, and at last committed suicide by cutting his throat with a razor.

Wherefore, make good use of your time, be occupied at something useful; learn or practise a regular trade, but take care how you spend the money you acquire by these means.

Now we come to—

§ 2.—The Regimental School.

What better use can a man possibly make of his time than in attending the Regimental School? Schools are provided by the Government for the purpose of educating every man in the Service so far at least as to enable him to read and write. Some soldiers say, "what is the use of going to school? I cannot learn." But this must be a mere feeling of discontent or disinclination. Such a man will go to school for a day or two, and then because he does not seem to be getting on, cease his attendance. But how can any man expect to learn to read and write in a few days? These two simple acquirements can only be gained by ordinary diligence and in a reasonable time.

Again, a soldier will say, when asked why he does not attend school: "What's the use?" My friends, it is of great use. First, with regard to mere worldly matters, how can a man who is ignorant of even what twice two will make, keep his own accounts? How does he know, when at the end of the month, he is called upon to sign his accounts whether they are correct or not? The Pay Sergeant may have made a mistake, to which every one is liable, and may have given him too much or too little. Too little is, I fear, the common mistake; if there be a mistake at all, it is seldom in favour of the poor ignorant soldier. How often do we see men in the most respectable and responsible positions tried by

Court-Martial for misappropriation of money? It is then evidently to the soldier's advantage to attend school, if he should only do so until he knows addition and subtraction. And when he has the opportunity of schooling *gratis*, why should he neglect it? Is it not better for a man to be at school improving himself than lying on his bed, or sitting about the barracks, smoking, drinking, or card playing? Lying in bed is very injurious to health, except at natural times, and doctors declare that often it is the only cause of Liver Complaint.

As for the vice of card-playing many and many a man has been ruined completely by acquiring in the Service this pernicious habit. It is all very well to say, " we are allowed to play." So far so good ; but for what and how are you allowed to play? Very simple ordinary games, and to these little objection can be made. But what does this play, as a rule, lead to? Without doubt to " *Gambling* ;" and when a man once gets a passion for gambling it is very hard to break him of it. The result is that if he should manage to obtain a position of trust, he sooner or later yields to a temptation to which that habitual passion exposes him, and is " weighed in the balance and found wanting." Now, you can surely see from these remarks, that it is much better for a man to attend school and try to improve himself, than to injure himself by other means such as idleness and gambling.

Never say you *cannot* learn. Every man can improve if he diligently applies himself to the task. The reward is very great. In the first place when a man is once able to read what an immense field of literature opens to his view! Writers of prose and poetry have worked for him, and from the depths of fertile imaginations have conjured up stories to delight him; have drawn pictures of home, which must touch his heart when far away from all he loves; have told stories of battles won and lost. And where is the soldier whose heart will not beat more quickly, and who will not himself feel a glow of pride, when he hears or reads of some heroic action?

When you are confined by sickness to your bed in hospital and there is nobody to take interest in you or to converse with you, reading will enable you to pass the time most pleasantly. When, through some misfortune, you are detained in the cells, you will find a book a pleasant and useful companion during the long lonesome hours you have to spend there. Above all, if you are in need of religious instruction, the power of reading your Catechism and Prayer-Book will be a great advantage. And when you have to write a letter about private affairs, you can do it yourself without asking another person to write for you.

But there is much more to be said on this subject. A man attending school gains, when qualified, a certain class of certificate, without which no one is eligible for promotion. And as every one should wish to get on and do the best for himself, and has, perhaps, dear relations at home whom he should assist, all who can, should attend school. Again, when a man has obtained the requisite certificate, which is sufficient for Non-Commissioned Officer's or Warrant Rank, (and in many cases even for a Commission) he has the opportunity of learning languages.

A Moonshee is provided who teaches him Hindustani, Marathi, Persian, and in many places also Arabic and Sanscrit. The most liberal rewards are granted by Government to soldiers for passing in each or any of these languages, and many have been able to leave India for England, Scotland, or Ireland, on what they have thus gained. So many, in fact, are the advantages, so many the situations to be obtained by being in possession of a 2nd Class Certificate of Education that it is really a great wonder that so few men, comparatively speaking, endeavour to obtain one.

Now listen to what an experienced schoolmaster has got to say regarding young illiterate soldiers, with whom he had a pretty extensive acquaintance in India for many years. He is of opinion that of no class of persons can it be said with greater truth that they do not know what they can do till they try. For the most part they have an aversion to school, thinking, no doubt, that there is no probability of their becoming sufficiently educated to enable them to rise in the Service. Some few there are of course, who are too indifferent to anything but their own immediate pleasure even to think of their own welfare in the future; and they only eat, drink, and sleep, bestowing an occasional malediction on the school. The school would be much better without these But the greater number—nearly all—possess a latent ambition which, with suitable opportunities, develops itself. The sense of the want of education depresses them, and generally their lack of confidence in their own powers indisposes them to make an effort Here, a little judicious advice and encouragement from the schoolmaster has usually a good effect. Many of them at this stage seek out the Schoolmaster of their own accord. If the schoolmaster is a man of experience and sympathy, the advice is given with encouraging words, which, [in hundreds of cases, have produced wonderful effects.

For the benefit of six-year men I will relate an instance, not of what *can be* done in six years, but of what *has been* done in that time. I know a man who entered the service quite illiterate, that is to say he knew his letters, and would perhaps make out the word " Cat," if he saw it in a book. I may say he knew nothing. Well, this man had been what is called a puddler, that is, he had been employed at smelting iron in South Wales, and had to work hard from boyhood for his livelihood. He was tall, well-formed, with a fine, open, sincere countenance, a splendid physique and not more than twenty years old. It was noticeable in this young man before very long that whatever he attempted he succeeded in accomplishing. As a recruit he was obliged to attend school which he hated; but after he had realized thoroughly that his future career depended upon his education, he set to work in good earnest, attended day and night, for there was a night school then, and before very long won a fourth class certificate, was made acting Bombardier and rough rider. I should have mentioned that this man belonged to the Royal Horse Artillery, and, as may be supposed by anyone acquainted with the interior economy of that distinguished corps, had his time—every hour in the day—pretty well taken up with multifarious duties. Yet he found time to take a 3rd. Class and not long after a 2nd. Class Certificate of Education, was admitted to be the best rider—and there were some good ones in the Brigade—and a crack swordsman. He competed at the annual Assault of Arms held at Poona on one occasion and took the first prize. A soldier of this stamp could not fail to be a marked man, and no one wondered when he became Sergeant, Battery Sergeant Major, and Brigade Sergeant Major in quick succession. Neither did any one grudge him his good fortune for he was a genuine, good fellow in all respects. "And what is he now?" you will ask. I will tell you. He is *Captain and Adjutant* of the Artillery Militia in

England. Now, this man had rendered his fortune secure in much less than six years although he entered the service under what must be admitted to be adverse circumstances as far as education was concerned.

To what was all this promotion due? To the efforts of the man himself you will say. True, but without the school, could he ever have obtained his present honourable position?

You may read another interesting case recorded in the Proceedings of the Royal Commission on Military Education presided over by Earl Dufferin in 1864, where an Army Schoolmaster in his evidence to the Commission on a point in connexion with the grievances of Military Schoolmasters said: " The other day I met and had to salute a Captain, to whom I had taught his letters as a recruit." Now, this was very creditable to the recruit and also to the Schoolmaster, but the latter thought that he himself was as useful in the service, and as deserving of promotion as the former.

Circumstances, no doubt, favoured the recruit; but, under no circumstances would he ever have attained to the rank of Captain without education. The moral of this is:—Qualify yourself educationally to be able to take advantage of circumstances. These two cases show what can be accomplished by men who avail themselves of the opportunities offered to them in the Service of bettering their condition.

At the same time remember that though a man may be slow, and even stupid, it is no excuse whatever *for his not trying* to get on. In the Parable we read that those who had used the talents were greatly rewarded, while he who had buried his talents was disgraced and punished. So shall it be when our time comes. To every one of us has been given a certain amount of ability; to one much, to another little; but the Almighty intends all to try and improve, and will bless our efforts. The Schoolmaster and his assistants are very ready to help all who go to school to get on. However *diligence* is assuredly the only thing any man needs.

Let then, each and all be advised to attend school, and try to make the best of the opportunity afforded. The way seems, and will be, hard at first; but march on—and conquer! Remember Charles Reade's definition of the word " Difficulties"—*Things to be Subdued*. Subdue and surmount them, and all will be well.

CHAPTER X.

The use a Soldier can make of his money.

No soldier I know of in the world gets so much pay as the British soldier in India. After defraying all his ordinary expenses and charges, a private soldier in the Infantry (and much more easily an Artillery man) can clear Rs 10 a month.

Now, what do they do with all this money? The greater part they spend in the canteen; and if they had three times as much as they have, they would spend it too in drink. There are some who spend it in the coffee-shop in getting extra comforts and even luxuries. Some put by their savings, or at least a portion of it in the Regimental Bank. Others spend a good deal in charities, sending every year a few pounds home to poor parents and friends. It is really remarkable, how certain soldiers deprive themselves of many comforts, pleasures and even necessaries simply with the intention of helping by their savings a poor relation at home.

In this regard the following edifying example of a son, who was good to his parents, will be a great encouragement to the charitable soldier. The General commanding a large military station in Germany had one day the Officers of the Garrison invited to dinner. Towards the end of the banquet he missed his watch and requested the gentlemen present to see whether it was on the table under some napkin.

They searched every corner, but the watch could not be found. The whole affair was disagreeable enough and looked very suspicious. The Officers rose, each turning his pockets inside out, to show that he had not taken the watch. However one young officer refused to show the contents of his pocket, and only assured the company upon his word of honor, that he knew nothing about the watch. Every other officer found this behaviour strange, and the party soon after broke up. That same evening the General sent for this officer at a late hour. "Excuse me," said he, "for causing you great annoyance at dinner. My watch is found. It had slipped through a hole in my pocket into the lower part of my coat. my servant has just found it. But may I ask you, Sir, why you refused to turn your pocket inside out as the other officers did?" The young gentleman blushed a little but answered: "Sir, I had my dinner (not your's) in my pocket, that is to say some bread and cheese. Your invitation, General, reached me in the middle of a walk I was taking, provided with my rations for the day." The General was surprised, for he could not understand, how an officer and gentleman with a liberal salary should live on bread and cheese.

"Are you a miser, or perhaps in debt?" asked the General, "What makes you live in that way?"

"No General," was the reply. "I come of poor parents, and my old mother has only a very small pension and is sickly. So I send her a little from time to time, and to get that little three times a week I eat bread and cheese only—a sweet sacrifice when I think I am thus able to assist my dear old mother. I intended to take a long walk this morning after parade, and so I took my rations in my pocket, when your invitation to dinner reached me, and as I told you I was in the middle of my expedition." Here the General wiped a tear from his eye and said with visible emotion. "Surely, you are a brave son! you must dine with me every day in future, in order that you may be able to send more to your good mother."

Young soldiers! What do you think of that example? You can imitate it with little trouble and so fulfil a filial duty to an old father or mother at home.

Besides this, especially if you have not to render pecuniary assistance to poor relations, you can make a very good use of the money you can spare by contributing in a liberal manner to subscriptions and collections for the chapel or for orphanages and other religious and charitable purposes.

The best plan to be adopted by a young soldier in this country will be to put some of the money he can spare in the Bank of the Regiment, and also some in the bank of Almighty God. The money in the Regimental bank will come handy to you when you are discharged from the Service. The money in the bank of Almighty God, that is to say, what you have spent for charitable and religious purposes, will come handy to you on your death-bed, nay, it will be paid back to you on the day of Judgment with more than double interest. Your good works, your charities, accompany you to the next world, and there you will find that you have laid up a treasure that will last for all eternity.

A soldier can easily have his money in both banks. Not long ago an Artillery man left the Service to take his pension in Australia. He had 1,700 rupees in the bank, and during his whole time out here he was known as a most regular and generous subscriber to the orphanages and chapels. He was not a miser, nor did he starve himself for the purpose of making money. The secret was that he always kept to himself and shunned the canteen.

Subscriptions to our orphanages have a very special claim on the Soldier. Some 30 years ago the chapels in the Bombay Presidency were few. Schools there were none, orphanages none, refuges for the poor, the sick, the widows none. The Protestants were then very active in establishing schools, and rich in subscriptions made in Europe and America and here too, and by the large grants of Government were able to receive our Catholic children into their institutions-—who there alas! became Protestants. Many a poor Irish Catholic in those times died in the hospital and on the battle-field, not knowing what would become of the orphans he left behind him. There being no arrangements then made for the education of Catholic children, the Commanding Officer of a regiment usually sent them to a Protestant orphanage, where they obviously lost their faith. The consequence was, that almost all the European and Eurasian young men and women, who frequented schools during that period, grew up staunch Protestants, many hating and despising the faith of their fathers. How many do we find in these days with Catholic Irish names who belong to the Protestant persuasion? These people, when young, were brought up in Protestant schools, and there lost their faith, not through any fault of theirs, but simply because they were educated in non-Catholic schools. The Protestant Byculla Schools in Bombay, the Lawrence Asylum on Mont Aboo and similiar institutions in other presidencies under the patronage of Government and wealthy military officials are able to boast of their propaganda among the Irish in India. The Catholic clergymen at that time were too few, too poor and destitute of influence to remedy the evil.

At last the ice was broken. The Catholic Soldiers, especially the brave Irishmen, responded in a very generous manner to their Chaplains' invitation by subscribing funds for building chapels and schools. One of the first monuments they erected in the Bombay Presidency was a Church in honor of St.

Patrick at Poona. An old record states, that every poor private Soldier paid Rs. 3 every month and non-commissioned officers in proportion to their rank. Eternal honour to the regiments stationed in the camp at that time. Their memory shall last for ever. There is now standing a splendid spacious church, of which it may truly be said, that every stone was purchased by the subscriptions of Soldiers. The names of these good men are not known to the world, and the privations and sacrifices which they imposed on themselves to pay their subscriptions may be hid under the cover of charity. Most of them are now in their graves, but Almighty God has registered their names in His Book of Life.

Similar efforts with the same success were made in other military stations, so that now there is a Catholic chapel in every camp.

It was not long before schools were built and orphanages founded for the children of soldiers who died in the country. Some help was after a while given by the Government.

In 1865 a remarkable fact occurred showing how Catholics, both civilians and soldiers, subscribed to the erection of two orphanages at Poona and Bombay One evening the members of the Confraternity were sitting in the compound of St. Patrick's Chapel, waiting for the commencement of the Rosary, when a carriage was seen driving past at a furious pace.

The horses had got quite unmanageable, and the driver had thrown the reins away. In the carriage two gentlemen were sitting pale, apparently in danger of being killed. Here one of the confraternity, an old Irish soldier, rushed forward to the horses, stopped them, got hold of the reins and brought the carriage to a stand still. The R. C. Chaplain, who had been looking on the scene, came immediately and invited the gentlemen to take some refreshments, which they did. They politely asked the Priest to be shown into the chapel, and they appeared much pleased with all they had seen and were, of course, very thankful for the real service and the kindness with which they had been received. Next day another carriage drove into the compound; it was that of Sir Bartle Frere, the then Governor of Bombay. He came to thank the Priest on behalf of those two gentlemen, one of them being his own Private Secretary. At his request, he was conducted to the chapel. The conversation led to the subject of schools. It must be noticed, that the erection of a school and orphanage at Poona had been contemplated long before, but from want of funds it could not be carried out, and Government had refused any grant-in-aid. The Priest, having explained these circumstances to His Excellency, was told to make a new application for the purpose. It was done, and the Governor in Council sanctioned the grant of a sum equal to what the Catholics should within a certain period subscribe. Now you should have seen the zeal of all Priests and people, especially of the Military Chaplains and soldiers in every camp. The latter subscribed thousands of rupees; some men as much as 20, 50 Rs., having drawn the money from the bank to meet the emergency. Within four months above 90,000 Rs. were subscribed, and the same amount was contributed by Government. Thus was the Bishop enabled to build St. Mary's Institution (St. Mary's College) in Bombay and the Convent at Poona. However, it was not enough to build the houses; the children had to be provided for too. In order to meet these expenses, monthly subscriptions were begun and still continue.

Such is the origin of the subscriptions to the orphanages, which are still made and published in the *Bombay Catholic Examiner*. The arrangement is this: With the sanction of the Commanding Officer the Priest submits the names of the subscribers to the Pay Master, who deducts every month the amount from the men's pay and sends it to the Priest to be forwarded to the Secretary of the Orphanages. A good plan, and perhaps the best that can be adopted. For when the men do not see the money, they are very content in this way to help in so good a work. When they have the money in their pocket, they do not like to part with it but spend it in drink; and many times it happens that, when the collection is made for ready money, they have none but have to wait for the next pay-day.

In certain stations Commanding Officers did not like the arrangement and refused permission to have these charities sent through the Pay Office. When the case was represented to the Commander-in-Chief, the following document was communicated:—

Adjutant-General's Office, Head-Quarters,
Poona, 13th December 1866.

Memo. No. 7306.

It has been brought to the notice of the Commander-in-Chief, that in some of the regiments of his Command, the subscriptions of Soldiers to schools or orphanages are allowed to be remitted by the Pay Master and shown in the men's accounts, whilst in others, the Commanding Officers do not permit the practice, under the impression that it is not in conformity with the regulations.

Sir Robert Napier sees much advantage in, and no objection to, permitting voluntary subscriptions for so desirable a purpose being passed through the account in the manner described.

By order,

(Signed) T. STOCK,

Adjutant-General of the Army.

CHAPTER XI.

§ 1.—The Soldier who wants to get married,

Since the introduction of the Short Service system, military marriages in India have been on the decrease. Several blocks of Patcheries are already empty; the number of children attending school is reduced in every station. Only now and then one meets with an old soldier's family, but they are soon going home to Europe. This reduction in the married quarters certainly saves expense to Government, and also saves the Quartermaster-General the trouble of providing for a soldier's wife and children in time of war. But whether the moral condition of the army is benefitted by it is quite another question.

What follows concerns chiefly the soldier who *can* and *will* get married, and is thinking of doing so. Is it better for him to marry, or to remain single?

(1). In a material or merely worldly point of view, we must admit that a married soldier in this country is well off. He has his own quarters in the Patcherie. Besides his own pay, he draws a "Family Allowance" of Rs. 8 per month for his wife, and Rs. 2-8-0 for each child. He has his rations for himself, and a portion for his family. He is supplied with furniture, oil-lamps, water, firewood; all he has to do with his pay is to keep himself and his family in clothing. There is a school, where his children are educated gratis; a hospital for any of the family who may be sick; medicines, the most expensive, wine if necessary, and everything else necessary in the way of diet,—in fact everything that can make one comfortable ; and when a husband with a large family keeps away from drink, his pay and allowance will go farther than a civilian's Rs. 100 per month, for the latter has to pay for everything out of that sum.

(2). In a religious point of view the married state may be recommended to those soldiers especially who have re-engaged, or who have cast their lot in this country. True, there are soldiers who lead a good moral life, and who resist all the temptations of the world, the flesh, and the devil. But are not these exceptional cases ? Look at the majority of cases, and consider the difficulty they experience in this regard. St. Paul says: "It is better to marry than to burn." And there are many in hell who would have been surely saved, if they had married.

Do not misunderstand me ! It is a dogma of the Catholic Church that preference must be given to the single state of life if embraced from religious motives. The state of virginity is more perfect than the married state. Hence the Church obliges her Priests, who daily offer up the pure sacrifice of the Lamb of God on the altar, to remain unmarried. The Holy Ghost in the Book of Wisdom (IV. 1.) bestows this praise on the unmarried state : "O how beautiful is a chaste generation with glory ! for the memory thereof is immortal." God honoured virginity by selecting a pure virgin for the Mother of His Son. The holy Fathers say that St. John was the most beloved disciple of Our Lord because he alone was a virgin. In heaven there will be a special distinction of the chaste: "They shall follow the Lamb, singing a song which others cannot sing," and those who have a place in the glorious resurrection, "shall neither marry nor give in marriage, but be like the angels in heaven."

The advantages of unmarried persons are mentioned by St. Paul in his Epistle to the Corinthians. "He who is without a wife," he says, "is solicitous for the things which belong to the Lord, how he may please God; but he that is with a wife is solicitous for the things of this world, how he may please his wife, and so he is divided (Cor. VII. 32). But yet it must be remembered that all these texts, all these praises of virginity, which extol the unmarried state of life only refer to those who out of love of God and for the sake of the service of God have chosen it. For, alas! there are but too many, who, in order to lead a free life, and to avoid the burden of Matrimony, remain single, and at the same time are given to debauchery of every description. Let them remember: "It is better to marry than to burn."

§ 2.—On Impurity.

After drunkenness, there is perhaps no sin so much indulged in as impurity. "Thou shalt not commit adultery." "Thou shalt not covet thy neighbour's wife." Thus run the sixth and the ninth Commandments. Strictly speaking, adultery means sexual intercourse between two, a single and a married person, or between two married persons, who are not husband and wife. But, as the 5th Commandment "Thou shalt not kill," forbids not only murder, but also fighting, quarrelling, injurious words, anger, hatred, revenge and scandal, so in like manner do the sixth and ninth Commandments forbid us not only all sins of uncleanness with another's wife or husband, but also every other kind of immodesty, as, in the first place, all impure thoughts, desires, or imaginations. When such cross your mind against your will, and you try to banish them, they are not sins, but are temptations; but as soon as you wilfully harbour them, or take pleasure in them, though only for a moment, you have committed a mortal sin against the ninth Commandment. You must make a distinction between bad thoughts and bad desires. It is a bad thought when you represent to your mind such objects and actions as are apt to excite lust; it is an impure desire, when you have a wish to see bad things, to hear or read about them, to do them either alone or with others. In confession you must say what was the object of these desires; because, according to the object, an impure desire may be simple fornication, or adultery, a sacrilege, or something worse.

Now, remember well, as long as you take no pleasure in these thoughts or desires and with God's help resist the temptations, there is no sin in them; but the moment you take pleasure in them, death enters your soul, you have committed a mortal sin against the sixth or ninth Commandment. Oh! how many entertain such bad thoughts and impure desires without even thinking that they are guilty of a grievous sin. How many souls are damned and are now enduring the pains of hell, simply for not having resisted such temptations! How many Christians make bad confessions and receive the Body and Blood of Our Blessed Lord unworthily, because they do not confess these *interior* sins in the proper manner! Pay then, in future, great attention to this point.

Secondly, to the same kind of sin belong unchaste looks. Our eyes are mirrors in which the soul sees the objects represented. When this mirror is in front of impure objects, representations fall on the soul and consequently impure feelings or motions must arise. For example, you see an impure picture, an indecently dressed female. What should you do? Turn your eyes away at once, and thus you are free from sin! But, when you fix your eyes on such objects, an impure lust is excited in you. Ah! in that case you have committed a sin of impurity. Hence you understand also what a great sin it is to keep and to show to others obscene pictures ; to appear before others without being properly dressed, and thus to become the cause of their souls being defiled.

Thirdly, filthy language. As for that you must know that not only those who use such language are guilty of sin, but also those who in any way encourage it by a smile; by enduring instead of stopping it when it is in their power to do so. Likewise, all loose talk, words of double meaning, indecent expressions, and immodest songs are sinful, and may be of awful consequence when children or other innocent persons are present.

Fourthly: The sixth Commandment also forbids all immodesty either with reference to yourself or another person, of the same or of a different sex, immodest kisses, unseemly amusements, such as often take place at the Regimental Theatre. It forbids every kind of flirtation. It forbids foolish attachment, indecorous levity, indecent jokes, improper familiarities with single or married persons.

Soldiers in the barrack-room have in this respect temptations of their own. As bad company leads them to drunkenness, so it leads them to fornication. Young men arriving in India should be very careful, and not follow the example of old soldiers who take a certain pride in showing them the wicked places in the bazaar. Whilst they boast of their own sins, they seem to strip themselves of that shame which God has given to all human beings as a defensive armour against the sin of impurity. One step leads to another, and the young soldier, who before barely knew such crimes by name, soon becomes enamoured of them and as bad as others. He cares not for prayer; he neglects his religious duties; he gives up his former devotions, and even if he be not addicted to drink, he will find it difficult to take and keep a pledge; impurity and intemperance are sisters. Thus it happens (too frequently, alas!) that he brings sickness on himself, and has his disgrace written on the hospital card. He wishes the Priest to pass by him—and, perhaps for the first time in his life, he is ashamed of his religion, and cannot bear the sight of his pastor.

But utterly false notions prevail among soldiers, and among civilians too, amongst persons even of the highest rank no less than among those of a humbler class, concerning the sin and shame of an immoral life. Many there are who walk and strut through life, most respectable in appearance, claiming and enjoying a spotless character, who are, in secret, and, in reality, *rotten* in this matter. So long as everything is concealed to the world, they are content. However there is one who sees and knows all your sins, your bad thoughts, your works of darkness. Almighty God will not only bring them to light on the day of Judgment, but will punish them with eternal fire if not repented of in time. Judge how grievous this sin is from the way he has, even in this life, punished it. For what sin but this did the Almighty inflict the great deluge on the world? Scripture mentions it in a few but strong words. (Gen. VI. 3.) "Men began to be multiplied on earth, and daughters were born to them. The sons of God, seeing the daughters of men, that they were fair, took to themselves wives of all they chose. And God said: "My spirit shall not remain in man for ever, because he is flesh." The sons and daughters of God were the descendants of the pious Seth; the children of men were the descendants of the impious Cain. These were guilty of impurity. It was the flesh which had corrupted them. God gave them time for penance, but they continued their wicked practices, and Noah alone found grace before the Lord, who commanded him to build the Ark for himself and his family. The flood came and all creatures, men and animals, that were not in the Ark, were destroyed.

What sort of sin is that which brought down that rain of fire from heaven, and turned the Paradise of God, which that region was, into the sea of death? I allude to the destruction of Sodom and Gomorrha. It was impurity, unnatural crimes. For these crimes God destroyed them in this manner. On the spot where the two cities formerly stood there is now a large lake, called the Dead Sea, because no living creature can exist in it. Such is the monument which God Himself has made for the whole world, even to this day, to show his anger against impurity.

What sin was it for which God himself punished with death in one hour 23,000 Israelites? Read the fourth book of Moses, Chapter 25, and there you will find that the Israelites cohabited with the daughters of heathens. The Lord in his anger said to Moses: "Take all the princes of the people, and hang them upon gallows against the sun, that my fury may be turned away." Every one had to kill his own neighbour. What a slaughter took place! What crying and lamentation was heard all over the camp, when the women saw their husbands executed, the children their parents, their brothers! How many noble chiefs were killed, how many families extinguished for ever! Such is the order and will of God, such the punishment he inflicts on fornication. Referring to this terrible fact, St. Paul writes: "neither let us commit fornication, as some of them committed fornication, and there fell in one day twenty-three thousand." (Epistle I. Cor. X. on the 9th Sunday after Pentecost). It would lead too far were we to mention all the temporal punishments which God has inflicted for that crime. Let us only turn our thoughts to the eternal punishment of hell.

Monsigneur de Segur has written a pamphlet entitled "Hell." He relates the following fact which occurred in 1848, concerning a lady who spent the winter season in London. She was rich, beautiful, and possessed of those manners which are sure to attract admirers. Among others a young nobleman paid her frequent visits, so frequent that she lost her reputation.

One night, about 12 o'clock, after reading as usual, in order to fall asleep, she put out the candle, and noticed a pale, yellowish flame that seemed to come from the door of the saloon. The door opened, and the young nobleman entered. Before she was able to say a word, he caught her by the wrist of the left arm, saying, "Madam, there is a Hell." The pain this caused her was so great that she fell senseless. As soon as she came to her senses again, it might be half an hour, she rang her bell. The servant came, and perceived the smell of fire. In fact from the door to the bed there were marks of fire, the carpet was burnt, and on her wrist there was such a deep burn, that the bone was all bare of flesh. The next day the lady heard that the unfortunate young nobleman was dead. He had expired on that night about 12 o'clock, having met with an accident whilst in a state of intoxication. The lady was still living in 1859, and always wore a broad bracelet on the wrist where she had received the terrible wound from hell. Ah, if these unfortunate persons had thought on the eternal punishment in hell! if they had feared hell! if they had compared the few moments of filthy pleasure with eternal punishment, surely they would have avoided sin. The thought of our last end should be always present to our mind. "For all thy works remember thy last end, and thou shalt not sin." (Ecc. VII. 40). This weapon should be used especially in temptations to impurity. The hermit Martinianus had already spent twenty-five years in the desert, practising the greatest austerities, when the devil tempted him to sin against the sixth

Commandment, and instigated a woman to go to his cell and tempt him to commit adultery. The Saint met the temptation by kindling a great fire, and thrusting his feet into it, and when they were nearly burnt, he exclaimed, "Ah, if I cannot bear this cold and lifeless image of hell, how shall I endure the reality"? This excited the woman to grief and repentance. She entered a convent at Bethlehem, and led a holy life until she died.

It is the common opinion of Holy Fathers and Spiritual Doctors that more souls go to hell for impurity than for any other sin. And indeed, what vice is so widely spread, and so much indulged in? What sin leads to such obduracy,—makes man so blind with regard to salvation? For what other sin are there so many occasions, so many excuses, such facilities? It can be committed in silence and darkness, alone, in company, anywhere. The thief, murderer or drunkard is abhorred and punished severely according to the laws of the country, whilst the votary of impure pleasure remains free and unnoticed, nay, even if known, he is not the less a welcome guest in the best society. But his judgment is only delayed. Death comes with all its terrors, and he is well aware of that sentence: "Begone, you cursed, into fire everlasting." He cannot expect a place among the chaste virgins in heaven, among those who have denied themselves the most innocent pleasures, and who have mortified their bodies. And for all eternity, for him there is the torment of hell-fire and the worm of conscience. "I tasted but a little honey, and lo! I burn."

You have now seen the extent or at least enough of this evil and its most ordinary consequences, temporal and eternal. "But how shall I be able to lead a pure, chaste life in the barracks? How can I resist all these temptations and avoid these constant occasions of sin?" you ask. Listen for a moment! It is *difficult* and arduous to overcome the enemy, but it is both easy and possible with the help of God.

You have perhaps six or eight years before you in this country, and during that time you must remain single. Priests, monks, and nuns make a vow of perpetual chastity, and the grace of their religious vocation makes it easy to keep that vow. But a soldier's life is so different from theirs. There is so much inducement and enticement in the barrack life to sin against the sixth Commandment and so little encouragement to lead a pure life. Yet God's grace is stronger than all temptation. He will give you ample grace to resist all these temptations. A soldier must, like every other Christian, avoid sins of impurity. If he leads a pure life under the circumstances in which he is placed, and if grace triumphs over lust, his reward will be great, nay, he will have greater merit in heaven than those who have been free from similar temptations. There are many who live untouched by the flames, though in the midst of a furnace. This is the greatest encouragement a soldier can have in his difficulties. Here are now a few counsels copied from the "Soldiers' and Sailors' Prayer Book," which will be of great use to you.*

(1.) *Fly the occasions.*—Without doing this, all else you do will prove of no avail; promises, tears, resolutions, confessions will be to no purpose. There are temptations which can be overcome only by grappling with the enemy, but with impurity we must pursue an opposite course. Here, in *flight* is the only means of securing victory. By flight the combat must begin, by flight it must be continued, in flight it must terminate. In this case, soldiers, bravery consists in fearing your enemy. Avoid licentious companions. You will soon and easily recognise them by their dissolute conversation. Keep aloof from persons of the other sex, whose presence may be an occasion of sin.

(2.) *Avoid idleness.*—An idle man stands all ready for Satan to make him fall into sin; he is his own first and most dangerous tempter. Be punctual in fulfilling the duties of your calling. Work and regular occupation are the best defences against the attacks of any passions.

(3.) *Frequent Prayer.*—To the shunning of occasions add frequency of prayer. Recommend yourself to God, and to the Blessed Virgin Mary, the

---
* To the Christian Soldier, Instruction, page 97.

Mother of Purity. When you are tempted, be careful not to notice the temptation, but immediately invoke the holy names of Jesus and Mary. Those sacred names put to flight every enemy of salvation, and extinguish the impure flames. If the temptation continues, persevere in prayer, and surely you will not fall. Practise some pious exercise in honour of the Blessed Virgin. For example, say three Hail Mary's in honour of her purity on rising in the morning, and on going to bed at night; recollect, especially the moment a temptation begins, to implore the assistance of Jesus and Mary; and, if you happen to commit any fault do not give way to discouragement; humble yourself before God, beg His pardon from the bottom of your heart, and use every means in your power to avoid new failings in the future.

Lastly be careful to frequent the Sacraments of Penance, and Holy Eucharist. Father Hunnold, a popular and very clever preacher in Germany, relates the following fact, which is very much to the point. A young man subject to temptations of impurity applied to a Priest for the purpose of obtaining his advice. He was told that the best thing for him would be to get married. So he got a wife, and settled down pretty comfortably, being now freed from all those terrible temptations which had made him miserable. A few years later his wife died, and then he was again troubled with the same temptations.

He went to a saintly Priest of the Society of Jesus, and explained his case. "The best thing you can do," said the Jesuit Father, "is to go once a week to Confession and Holy Communion." The poor man, in his disturbed state of mind first thought that he was not worthy of receiving the Holy Sacraments so often, but he tried it, as he was advised to do. Strange to say it cured him, and he got rid of all his temptations.

Some time ago an old soldier of the 4th King's Own Regiment told a similar story of himself. During two years he was a weekly communicant, and he asserted that there was no greater help to a frail man to keep away from sin, than this pious practice. "No temptation to get drunk, or to commit a sin of impurity gets hold of me," he said, "when I remember that I receive every Sunday our Blessed Lord. If I should leave off these my devotions, I should not have strength to resist the temptations which surround me."

§ 3.—Choice of a Wife.

Now the soldier who has considered before God, and come to the conclusion that he should marry, and can obtain permission in order to have his wife and family on the strength of the Regiment, is often at a loss whom to choose for his companion.

There are Native girls, Eurasians, Europeans, Catholics and Protestants; children grown up in the Patcheries, and others who have been educated in a convent school. Where is the advantage in each of these? Where is the disadvantage? If a soldier or a pensioner has made up his mind not to remain in the country, he should marry no one but a European, because plainly it will be a great treat for her to leave with him for Europe. If he settles in India for good, his choice may fall on a Native or Eurasian,—he may lead a happy and contented life with such a one.

Some soldiers contract marriages with Natives whilst serving without permission from the authorities; but when discharged they do not like to leave their wife and children behind, more particularly when the wife has always been faithful to her husband and a kind mother to her children. Other soldiers, who have contracted marriages in a similar manner, go home when their time is in, and are cruel enough to leave their little family behind without any means of support. A European soldier who marries a Native with or without permission should earnestly consider what he is doing.

There are alas! too many instances of the misery and poverty which have been brought on unfortunate women, who have been left behind without protection or support by Europeans leaving for home and who have never been heard of since they embarked.

Others who remain single whilst in the Service and take their pensions in the country because they have no friends at home, contract marriages with Natives, as much for the sake of companionship, as anything else. In most cases there is not more luck than love in such unions. The husband, although his means are small, perhaps one shilling a day, is usually a reckless sort of man who, on the day he draws his three months' pension gets drunk, and spends the greater part of his money. In a very few days the whole of his pension is gone,—he ill-treats his wife, and starves her well during that time—and at the end of it he has nothing to live on but his wits; and we know what they are, and what they will bring in until the next quarter's pension becomes due. These are the sort of Europeans who are to be seen knocking about the streets of Bombay and Poona, never employed, and, a disgrace to their nation and colour. No doubt those men who are often good clerks or skilfull tradesmen, had they been discharged in Europe, could have mixed with their own class of people, and would have been in a better condition than they are in India, where the climate is over-powering, as also is the bottle. They should never have been married in this country to a Native woman.

Not that all pensioners are of this stamp. There are many of them who have contracted marriages in India with Natives living very respectably, and are worthy of notice. They do not like being idle, and get employment here and there. They put their earnings to very good use, build a cottage for themselves in some suitable place, and lay by a little store for a rainy day. They give a good example to their Native wives, and in return these are faithful and careful. They are to be seen on Sunday respectably dressed, going together to their place of worship. They join in prayer every night before going to bed, and invoke the blessing of the Almighty, which cannot fail to descend on such a family. Their means are perhaps scanty, but with care and sobriety they live comfortably, and bring up their children in the fear and love of God, always glad of the counsel of their Priest, who takes the greatest interest in their welfare, spiritual and temporal. In such cases, and under such circumstances an old soldier is quite happy with his Native wife.

There are also advantages and disadvantages in marrying a European wife. The advantages are that should he be permitted to do so, he can go home with his family when his time has expired, or when sickness makes a change to Europe imperative. In the Patcherie he will more easily keep peace with his neighbours, and his wife will not be insulted, as a Native or Eurasian woman, alas! too frequently is. In fact he will be better able to mix with his countrymen, supposing his European wife is a good, respectable, quiet person. But if she be not such, it is a great disadvantage to the soldier married to a European.

There are two classes of European girls in this country from which a soldier may choose a wife : viz., the children of soldiers brought up in the Patcherie, and those who have been educated in a Convent. The former class look out for a Non-Commissioned Officer; a private soldier need not apply for them. They must have a sergeant, a sergeant major, a conductor, or some one higher still. Their parents will never allow them to marry a man without chevrons. This is one of the principal causes of the mixed marriages so frequent in the army. For, as there are only a few Catholic Non-Commissioned Officers in the station, the Protestants who propose for such girls usually marry them.

There is a very bad custom prevalent in the Patcheries when a man is courting. The father, and perhaps also the mother, of a marriageable girl may be fond of the bottle, as is too often the case. Young men are always welcome in their quarters so long as they bring drink with them. It is a real fact that matches are made up, and are again broken off on this account. Thus when a young sergeant thinks he is quite sure of getting married to a girl and has spent much money in supplying her parents with drink, he is suddenly told that she will get married to another man, with whom the same game has been played probably to result in a similar disappointment.

It is not the fault of the girl, but that of the parents that promises of marriages are thus made and marriages actually contracted with men of a different religion, and perhaps even of a bad moral character, European girls born in India and brought up in the Patcheries often inherit the vicious habits of their parents, and turn out to be drunkards, licentious, careless about religion, fond of pleasure, dress and dances. They are careless and lazy, and neglect their household affairs, and are often a real encumbrance to their husbands. Of course there are exceptions; but any Non-Commissioned Officer (private soldiers have no chance) should think twice before he proposes for such a girl.

In our Convent Schools you find a wholly different class of girls. Those who can get married from out of a Convent are generally orphans. The nuns have taken the place of their parents, and with this duty also a grave responsibility,—the settling them in life. Most of them have been in these religious houses from their earliest years, and know comparatively little about the world. They have been under the careful supervision of the nuns all day long; they have received a good religious and secular education; they have been taught how to fulfil their religious duties, how to go through their devotions, and so on. As a rule, they are innocent and good. Now, when they have attained the age of 16 years, and the Government allowance is stopped, they may remain for another year or so in the Convent, making themselves useful as teachers or monitresses. If they have no vocation for a Religious Order, if they cannot go into service, nor do anything for themselves in another way, they are the persons to whom a European might get married.

Many happy matches have been made with such girls. The good example they give to their husbands has had the most beneficial influence on them, and there are, at the present time, many soldiers and civilians residing in India who can bear testimony to the text of Scripture (Prov. XIX. 14.) : " Houses and riches are given by parents, but a prudent wife is properly from the Lord," also (Prov. XVIII. 22): " He that has found a good wife has found a good thing, and shall receive a pleasure from the Lord."

§ 4—On Mixed Marriages.

A Catholic intending to marry should above all other considerations fix upon a virtuous person who is of his own religion. A marriage contracted between a Catholic and a Protestant is called a *Mixed Marriage*.

Our Holy Church, from the beginning, has at all times disapproved of mixed marriages, and, except to avoid greater evils and under certain conditions, has never tolerated them.

St. Ambrose says : " Take heed, not to marry a pagan, or Jew, or heretic." With this great Doctor all the other holy Fathers agree, nay the whole Church in the decisions of her Councils uphold him. The synod of Elvira in Spain decreed in 340 that parents, who allow their daughters to marry heretics should do penance for the space of five years.

The Popes, particularly since the so-called Reformation have always spoken in the severest terms against such marriages, and have only permitted them, when they have permitted them, to avoid greater evils.

In the old times before Christ God Himself forbade such marriages. For when He introduced His people into the Holy Land, He laid the strongest injunctions on them never to intermarry with the pagan people of that country. On this subject read (Deut. VII. 2.): "Neither shalt thou make marriages with them; thou shalt not give thy daughter to his son, nor take his daughter for thy son, for she will turn away thy son from following me." Seductions of this kind actually took place, for after the death of Joshua the children of Israel dwelt in the midst of the Chanaanites and they took the daughters of the land to wives . . . . and they did evil in the sight of the Lord and they forgot their God (Judges VI. 6).

King Solomon, though so great in wisdom, fell into sin in this very way. For, as it is related in 3 : Kings, XI. 1. "Solomon loved many strange women......of the nations of which God had said to the children of Israel: You shall not go into them, neither shall any of them come into you. For they will most certainly turn away your hearts to follow their gods......And when he was now old, his heart was turned away by women to follow strange gods."

This danger of losing the faith is one of the first reasons why the Catholic Church is so opposed to mixed marriages. The true faith is the most precious treasure a Christian has, the indispensable condition of our eternal salvation. Wherefore the Church so anxiously watches over her children, and so zealously guards against all dangers of her children losing their faith. Such a danger exists in every mixed marriage. Familiar intercourse with persons of a false religion naturally, and even necessarily, tends to undermine the principles of the true faith; and where is intercourse so familiar and so close as that between husband and wife?

You will say that an Irish Catholic runs no such risk when he marries a Protestant. Nay; but how many lamentable cases have occurred, in which the Catholic party has become first indifferent to religion, and has ended by losing his faith. Commissioned Officers, come of the best Catholic families and who had received the best of education in the most religious manner, have, by marrying Protestant ladies, come to all but an open abandonment of their faith, and have, at all events, given up the most obligatory of their religious duties, and given the greatest possible scandal. The society, the Protestant relatives of the wife, the whole atmosphere in which they lived, brought on the strong temptation of human respect and made them shy, and soon ashamed, of Catholic practices. In conversing with friends and relations everything is avoided which may betray a Catholic; the sign of the cross is not made any longer when grace is said at dinner time; the days of fasting and abstinence belong to the past; there is no more Confession nor Holy Communion; the sacrifice of the Mass is neglected; and perhaps to please the Protestant party occasional visits are made to the Protestant Church. The service. the sermon there is found to be not at all so bad, not by any means in bad taste,—very like Catholic service perhaps in these days of Ritualism, and so the visits continue until the last spark of the true faith is extinguished.

And what about the children? The proper, thorough Catholic education of the offspring of a mixed marriage is in most instances difficult if not impossible, but how can it be otherwise? This is another, and if possible a still greater reason why such alliances should be avoided. Let us suppose that the Protestant husband and wife are not bigotted and an agreement to have been made, that all the children should be baptized and educated in the Catholic faith. The zeal of the believing parent will no doubt be able to do a great deal in the matter. But after all the whole education should be the work, not of the one, but of the two— of father and mother. Or, what is to be expected of children who hear one thing from one parent, and at all events see the contrary in the other? who see the Catholic mother reverence religious practices, while the Protestant father, if he does not ridicule, at least shows not the slightest reverence for them.

We find a remarkable comparison of such poor children in 2 Esdras XIII. 27. When the Jews returned from captivity, Nehemias their leader saw some of the Jews who had married strange women, and what was the consequence? "Their children," says he, "spoke neither the language of the father nor of the mother, but half of the one and half of the other," for which Nehemias chid them and laid his curse upon them, showing them from the example of Solomon the great evil they had done, and the danger they ran, and concludes: "Shall we also be disobedient to do all this great evil, to transgress against our God and marry strange women?" Upon this text a renowned English Catholic Bishop justly remarks. "How often does experience show, that the children of parents who are of different religions, speak neither the language of the one nor of the other in religious matters."* In fact, it happens but too frequently that the offspring of mixed marriages become indifferent about religion. Can any state of soul and heart be worse for salvation? And if the Catholic parent dies and the Protestant surviving parent, and Protestant relations or guardians get hold of the children, will they be brought up in the Catholic faith? Some years ago a Catholic Irish soldier who had married a Protestant, the latter having agreed that all the children should be educated in the Catholic faith, died in the hospital at Poona.

---

* The Sincere Christian, by the Right Revd. Dr. George Hay.

He died leaving two children, and his dying request was that they should be sent to the Convent. They remained only a few months there: the mother soon married again, and this time a Protestant. They removed the children from the Convent and made them Protestants in spite of all her engagements and of all the affectionate promises she had made to her husband on his death-bed.

Ignorant and indifferent Catholic girls in this country sometimes get married to Protestants in the Protestant church, and then there is no agreement made regarding the religion of the future offspring. By doing this, they are guilty of a very grievous sin. The first child is born and baptized by the Protestant minister. Then she comes to chapel to receive the Catholic blessing after childbirth. The Priest must refuse to church her, and she, disheartened, keeps away from the Catholic place of worship altogether and neglects her religious duties, in complying with which, she was, perhaps, before her marriage very regular. Yes, one meets, and *often* meets with cases as strange as this, and even stranger. A girl will wish to go to the Sacraments meaning to do so, and that just before she enters on a course like this. If she does not become a Protestant she is certainly on the way to become one and to die an unhappy death. How terrible will be her portion on the day of Judgment! She will see her children again, and also her children's children to the last generation, but without the true faith and she is the first cause of it; she is the first link of that unhappy chain now standing on the left side among the damned.

But the trials and troubles of a mixed marriage begin in this world. Peace and happiness are the greatest blessings on husband and wife. Now what is the peace, what the happiness which is not founded on religion? They are hollow and false, with no more substance in them than in a dream. Are they to be found when the parties are of different religions, the one the true, and the other a false one? How many sneers and slanders is the believing party often exposed to hear? But even supposing there are none, can any one imagine intercourse more dreary than that from which everything touching our religion is excluded? And yet this exclusion is necessary to secure anything like peace in the family. There must be a common agreement to be indifferent. What difficulty does a Catholic woman find in observing the rules and practices of her religion in such a case? Husband and wife do not pray together, they have not the same source of religious consolation, and where is that sweet hope that they will find one another again in a better life?

CHAPTER XII.

§ 1.—The Soldier's Wife & Life in the Patcherie.

Once married, and quartered in the Patcherie you must remember in the first place that husband and wife are to live together in peace, they must love one another and always be faithful to the promise they make at the step of the altar—" until death does part them." Matrimony is according to the intention of Christ (who raised it to the dignity of a Sacrament), a representation of that union which exists between Christ and his Church. But this union is a peaceful one and a true manifestation of natural love. The heavenly bridegroom remains with his immaculate bride even in time of trouble and persecution, and nothing can prevail on the Church to forsake Him. So, in like manner, a husband must love his wife, and both must live together in peace.

Indeed on the good understanding between husband and wife depends the whole prosperity of the family. To this we may apply the words of the Psalmist: " Behold, how good and pleasant it is for brethren to dwell together in unity...for there the Lord gives blessing and life for evermore." (Psalm 132). And the Holy Ghost says in the book of Sirach; " With three things my spirit is pleased, which are approved by God and men ; the concord of brethren, the love of neighbours ; and man and wife that agree well together." (Eccl. XXV. 12.) Nothing is more edifying than to see married people leading a peaceful, contented life. It makes them happy even in trials and troubles. When Elkana, of whom we read in I Kings I. 8. asked his wife Anna, why she told him that she was sad, and she told him that it was on account of her not having children, he replied, "Am I not better to thee than ten children?"

But, when there is neither peace nor love between married people, they have a real hell on earth.

Secondly, they should edify each other by a pious life. Of the first Christians Tertullian writes: "They pray and fast together. They appear together in Church and at the Lord's table." The influence a good husband has over his wife in this respect is very great, and a wife can do a great deal by word and example to encourage her husband in the service of God. Many men have become excellent Christians by marrying a good religious wife, who has kept them away from drink and bad company and has induced them to be regular in complying with all their religious duties. Such, however, is not the case in every family. The spirit of religion, of prayer, and piety is banished. The name of the devil is oftener heard than that of God. One party wishes for the other's death, and so they give each other the worst example.

It is the husband's duty to support his wife according to his means; or as St. Chrysostom says, "Husbands, take care of your wives, in the same manner as Christ takes care of his Church." It is the wife's duty to obey her husband in all that is not sin, and to look after her husband's affairs. St. Paul writes in the 5th Chapter of his Epistle to the Ephesians: "Let women be subject to their husbands as to the Lord. For the husband is the head of the wife as Christ is the head of the Church." This subordination of woman has its foundation in the natural order itself. God made Adam first, and then formed Eve out of one of Adam's ribs, and only for the sake of Adam, in order that he might have a companion. Another reason for woman's subordinate place is to be found in the sentence God pronounced against Eve. She had believed the serpent, which told her to eat of the forbidden fruit in the garden of Eden. But God decreed in punishment for that sin: "Thou shalt be under the power of thy husband, and he shall rule over thee."

From this it follows that a good wife should obey her husband, and respect him like Christ, who is the head of the Church. For example, when the husband tells his wife to hold her tongue, she must be silent; when, for any good reason, he wishes her to stay at home, she must not go out; when he is against her contracting friendship with certain people, she must avoid them; and so on. She must be obedient to her husband in all that is not sin. St. Peter in the third Chapter of his first Epistle says the same. "Let wives be subject to their husbands;

that if any believe not the word, they may be gained without the word, by the conversation of the wives......whose adorning let it not be the outward plaiting of the hair, or the wearing of gold, or the putting on of apparel......for after this manner heretofore also the holy women, hoping in God, adorned themselves, being subject to their husband."

Concerning the affection and love of wives towards their husbands, a curious but true fact is mentioned in the history of Bavaria. A place called Weinsberg was besieged by the German Emperor Conrad, and compelled to surrender. All the women of Weinsberg held a meeting in order to consult as to the best means of saving their husbands, for the order was that they should all be put to death. So they sent a petition to the Emperor, beseeching him to allow them to leave the city with all that they could carry on their backs. Permission was granted. The Emperor himself came to have a look at the procession as he wanted to know how much they could carry. Too strange, but quite true. The gates opened, and first came the Duchess with her husband, the Duke, on her back. After her came all the noble ladies, followed by the poor, all carrying their husbands on their backs. At this sight the Emperor could not help giving vent to his feelings. Tears rolled down his cheeks, and he spared the city on that account.

Our Patcheries alas! but too frequently present totally different scenes of matrimonial love. The chief cause of family quarrels is drink on the part of the husband, and bad temper on the part of the wife, and when the latter also is fond of the bottle (as she often is), when she neglects her household affairs and goes round the Patcherie telling stories (as too many do), complaining of her husband, making rather free with other men or abusing her neighbours, then indeed it is a bad case.

At the same time a married man must not make a bad use of his authority. His wife is not his servant, but his companion. St. Augustine beautifully remarks that God has made the wife out of the rib of Adam, in order to show that she has the next place to himself in his heart. Wherefore, "husbands, love your wives, as Christ has loved His Church."

Let husband and wife walk together hand in hand through this stormy life and bear with patience their cross, for difficulties will not be wanting. Many before getting married have fancied they would make a bed of roses for themselves, but after their honeymoon was over, they discovered that there were no roses, but only plenty of thorns.

The best advice that can be given to young married women in the Patcherie is: "Do not make too free with your neighbours, in order to have peace with them." Most quarrels and actual fights originate from intimate friendships that had been formed once and broken off subsequently. Hence the most disgusting scenes and all the trouble of the Commanding Officer in the Orderly Room. Here is an illustration of this truth.—

§ 2.—Three days in the Patcherie, after arrival from Europe.

India is one of the best countries in the world for Soldier's wife. Mrs. O' Shaughnessey was married at home to a private and used to work as a washerwoman to earn wherewith to support her family. They are now quartered in the patcherie. The first day after her arrival, Mrs. Jones comes to see her, a very wise, good person; her only fault is that she takes a drop too much now and again.

Mrs. O'Shaughnessey does not drink; she keeps the children nice and clean, though her husband Patrick is fond of a drop at times. Twelve o'clock strikes, Canteen opens, Mrs. Jones enters.

"Good day; I have heard you arrived yesterday and come to see you. I am Mrs. Jones, the wife of your Colour Sergeant. How is your husband and the children?"

"Quite well," says Mrs. O'Shaughnessey, "it is very kind of you, indeed, to come and see me."

Mrs. Jones takes a survey of the house, and gives an account of other women of the Company, to whom she would not be seen speaking. This done, she inquires if Mrs. O'Shaughnessey never drinks her porter.

"No, Mrs. Jones, sure the children want some clothes on arriving in India, and I want some for myself, and so I cannot afford anything for drink."

"Nonsense, woman," says Mrs. Jones, "what do you want dressing the children up in this hot climate! See my little fellows running about without shoes or stockings, it makes them hardy,"—and to substantiate her argument, she calls out: "Harry, come here my boy." And there runs up a little urchin, quite dirty, with a part of his shirt hanging out of his trousers.

"A fine boy, God bless him! How old is he"? asks Mrs. O'Shaughnessey.

"Five years next June," says Mrs. Jones, "and he is very clever too; he goes to the Canteen every day and brings his mama's porter—he does. "Go now, my boy and let Mrs. O'Shaughnessey know, how quick you can fetch a can-ful." Here, the child is despatched on his errand.

"You would not believe, Mrs. O'Shaughnessey, but it is the only thing that keeps the life in me in this country—and sure, my poor old man says the same—sure, he is the good husband."

In this way the women discoursed, until the arrival of little Harry with the long sleever.

"Now you must have a little drop of this with me," says Mrs. Jones.

"Oh, I declare, Mrs. Jones, I would not. I never drank porter in my life."

"Do not be a fool, woman," says Mrs. Jones, "just try that little drop, and you will see, how nice it is." Mrs. O'Shaughnessey takes the glass and drinks a little, whilst Mrs. Jones does justice to hers, and refills it again, remarking that the measurement was short to-day. Here she calls out for Harry and scolds him for not seeing to the measurement.

"It is the fault of the Canteen boy" says he, "he never fills the pots for the women."

"Oh, I will let that drunken blackguard know that I am Mrs. Jones, the Colour Sergeant's wife. Now, run off my child and call for Mrs. O'Shaughnessey's porter. You have no objection Mrs. O'Shaughnessey, to my getting yours?"

"Oh, not in the least, Mrs. Jones, you can have it every day for that matter."

Here the little fellow is despatched again, in the heat of the day without shoes on his feet, to gratify the appetite of his old drunken mother. However before starting Harry says: "Mama, I am hungry." "Now go," says his mother, "you are always hungry; make haste, and when you come back I will give you some bread."

At this the young fellow departs. quite content, and both women continue their conversation. Mrs. Jones takes up her glass, eyes it and drinks off the remainder. By this time little Harry arrives with the second 'attack' (as they call it), saying, "now Mama, I want the bread."

"Oh Harry, you are a good boy, Mama's own pet, go up to the house and you will find some bread in the cupboard."

Here he toddles and finds some stale bread, quite hard, and brings it to his mother saying: "It is too hard, I want some butter." "Go" says she, "you always want butter; how can I afford to buy butter, and besides this it would make you bilious."

"Now, Mrs. O'Shaughnessy, you have not emptied your glass, you do not know what is good for you; you must have another drop of it." So the glasses are filled again and the conversation is turned into another channel.

"We will have a Good Templars' dance to-morrow night; Mrs. O'Shaughnessey, are you a good dancer?"

"I can't dance, Mrs. Jones, but I am quite a stranger here, and besides we do not belong to the Society, as my husband likes a drop now and again."

"Oh, that does not matter," says Mrs. Jones, "my old man is at the head of it, under the Reverend Mr. Brislaw, and I will get you an invitation for the dance, and I shall be glad to see you along with me."

"I cannot give you an answer, Mrs. Jones, till I see my husband."

"Oh, you fool, Mrs. O'Shaughnessey, why do you allow your husband to control you in these little matters of pleasure! I would not let my old man interfere with me, every one knows that!"

By this time Mrs. Jones had got rid of the contents of her glass and has betaken herself home to receive her husband at dinner and to have another glass with him. For she did not relish the two previous quarts, saying the porter was not so good to-day as yesterday, and the Canteen boy must be at once removed.

"I have seen Mrs. O'Shaughnessy to-day; she is a very nice sort of a person, and neither herself nor husband drink, and no doubt he would answer you in the Canteen as barman, and would not be so sharp in detecting you adding a bottle more water to the liquor."

"Yes, dear," says Sergeant Jones, "I think that would be a good plan and decidedly to my advantage."

After dinner the woman went over to Mrs. O'Shaughnessey to tell her she had done her a good turn, that her husband was to be barman of the Canteen next day at 12. Patrick O'Shaughnessey had just come home and was delighted at the news, but Mrs. Jones gave him also her lesson regarding her porter and that he was to fill her pot up to the brim. Before leaving she warned Mrs. O'Shaughnessy to be ready for the dance. After she had gone away Patrick asks his wife: "What dance is this that Mrs. Jones talks about?"

"It is the Temperance dance" says she, "and Sergeant Jones is the headman."

"A fine headman" replies Patrick, "with half a bottle of blue rum in his stomach."

Next day, at 12 o'clock Patrick O'Shaughnessy took charge of his new appointment as waiter in the Canteen, and put a heap of porter in Mrs. Jones' can. When the Canteen was closed and Patrick came home his wife asked him, how he liked the job.

" Oh, very well indeed, said he, I got four quarts for nothing."

" But why did you not bring some porter home for dinner ?"

"How was I to bring it, woman, I had no can."

" Well then," says she, " I will go to the bazaar at once and get one like that of Mrs. Jones."

So she goes to a tin-man's shop and observes a long tin can, about a foot and a half long.

" What is the price of a tinpot ?" The Bora answered, he had no tinpots to sell. " But what do you call this thing ?" " Mam," says the Bora, " we call it long sleever, and the price is 3 annas."

Here Mrs. O'Shaughnessy remarked that it seemed larger than Mrs. Jones' one. " No Mam," said the Bora, "I make Sergeant Jones' sleevers *all same size.*" So she paid down the amount and took the commodity, quite proud (and yet a bit ashamed too) that she would be as good as any of them now, and that her husband could supply her with a drop every day.

A 7 o'clock the Canteen opened for the night issue. Patrick went away to his business, and his wife commenced dressing for the dance. In company of Mrs. Jones she went to the Temperance Hall. Sergeant Jones was at the door, took her by the hand and introduced her as a new member to Revd. Mr. Brislaw, who was very glad to see her. After Mrs. O'Shaughnessey took her seat, the Revd. Gentleman gave some instructions to all present and then the dance commenced. Mrs. Jones did not dance, but she contented herself over a glass of wine, which is the only drink allowed the "Ladies" as they call them.

Mrs. O'Shaughnessey danced, and as after every dance she was invited to take a little wine, and took it, she got before long very talkative, and was pretty tight, as they say; for the less elegant word is *tipsy*. The dance broke off at 12 o'clock.

Mrs. Jones also was pretty merry, and after arriving at home she would not let her friend go without giving her a little drop to kill the worm before going to bed.

Mrs. O'Shaughnessey felt very queer next morning, and confessed to her husband the state her head was in.

"I cannot look at breakfast this morning."

Here Patrick's new appointment becomes useful.

"Sure," he said, "last night I thought it would be so, and I have managed to secure a drop for the morning."

"Oh, God bless you Paddy, sure you always think for one." For the first time in her life Mrs. O'Shaughnessey becomes a victim to the bottle. She got her peg, and then was able to take her breakfast.

It was about 9 o'clock in the morning when the Catholic Chaplain went around the married lines, to ascertain, if there were any belonging to him among the new comers that had arrived from Europe. Some of the other women informed him of a Mrs. O'Shaughnessey being a Catholic. She was just standing at the door.

"How do you feel after your voyage from England?" asks the Priest.

"Quite well, Father, and so are the children. Come here, Paddy and Micky—they are rather dirty, I have had no time to clean them since I came, and I have no servant to assist me." The Revd. Gentleman remarked, that a basin of water and a scrub would do their faces no harm.

"Where is your husband, Mrs. O'Shaughnessey?"

"Sir, he is gone to the Canteen, as he was appointed barman by Sergeant Jones, our Colour Sergeant, who is very kind to us and so is his wife. She invited us to the Temperance Ball last night."

"Very kind of them," says the Priest, "and how did you enjoy the dance? Who was there?"

Here poor Mrs. O'Shaughnessey in her simplicity lets the cat out of the bag. When she had done, the Priest smiled gravely: " So, Mrs. O'Shaughnesse, you have no servant to assist you, you have had a time to clean your children, but you find time to go to the dance and stop there till morning. No you must drop this sort of amusement and also te your husband to give up that job in the Canteen an labour honestly to maintain his little family. Ser him to my house when he comes home."

" I will, Sir," said Mrs. O'Shanghnessey, and turned in with a long red face. The first thing that caught her eye in the room was the long sleever, which she had purchased the previous evening. Alas! she says to herself, after paying my 3 annas for that misfortunate article—and I shall never have the pleasure of using it? Never mind; it must, it must go. I have to give it up, but I will have it full *one* day at least, please God.

Patrick did not return till after Canteen closed, so that she was able to make use of the sleever for the first time.

Mrs. Jones was sick after the night's gorge, and did not call on Mrs. O'Shaughnessey at 12 o'clock, as usual. There was rather a great uproar at the Canteen, and Patrick O'Shaughnessy got insulted by half a dozen old soldiers for taking the place of their old friend, and several remarks were passed about his wife and Colour Sergeant Jones dancing at the Temperance Hall. When he came home his wife could see by his face that something had happened.

"What is the matter?" says she, as they sat down to dinner.

"I have been insulted" was Patrick's reply, "and so have you been for going to that d......d dance." After hearing all about the affair from him, she commenced about the Priest.

"Well," says her husband we will go and see him. In the evening they both went with the children, who were now clean and neatly dressed to the Reverend Father's house to hear what he had to say to them. The Priest saw them coming and went to the door to receive them. On casting an experienced eye on them he noticed that there was a decided change.

"Did you give any liquor to your wife this morning?" asks the Priest.

"A little drop, Sir."

"Yes, and you would give her a bigger drop tomorrow, and drop by drop she would become as big a drunkard as Mrs. Jones, the woman who sought her destruction."

"Now, go and give up that appointment as barman in the Canteen. I expect you both at your duty next Sunday, and to see your children clean at school in future."

On their return home Patrick gave up the Canteen; Mrs. Jones was very angry and said that these Irish know nothing about Society, and do not read the Bible —and what not.

Twelve months afterwards Patrick was a full Corporal and doing well, as also were his little family.

It is very much to the advantage of married people in the Patcheries, when the Officer Commanding a Battery or Company takes interest in their welfare, especially also when Officers' wives visit these quarters. So long as religious affairs are not touched upon and a lady is impartial to all alike, the married people, especially the women will be greatly benefitted by it. However, there are certain women who impose on charitable and kind ladies in order to get something for themselves or their husbands—some staff appointment or promotion. They tell stories about their neighbours, which, of course, come to the ears of the Commanding Officer and may do great harm. The worst is, when they are seen running to the Commanding Officer to obtain through the influence of his wife a favour which they generally make a bad use of afterwards. Many a lady has had sad experiences in this respect, and has been disappointed at seeing that all the troubles she has taken to make the married people and their children comfortable and content has been in vain.

The Military Chaplain also who occasionally visits the Patcheries finds himself in presence of difficulties which baffle all description. It is a common complaint that soldiers' wives do not always come to Mass on Sunday, nay, some of them are never seen in Chapel, except perhaps on Christmas at midnight

Mass. The excuses they make to the Priest are manifold. But, when a tea-party comes off or a theatrical performance, or a dance, they have time to leave the house in spite of all their difficulties. It is not the care they have to take of little children, nor bad health, nor want of decent clothing which can prevent them from going to these places of amusement. Thus they commit a mortal sin every Sunday when through their own fault Mass is neglected. They give bad example to their children. They remain ignorant, as they never hear a sermon, and deprive themselves of the choicest blessings of Heaven.

CHAPTER XIII.

The Soldier's Children.

One of the most important duties married people have to fulfil is the education of their children. Nobody will deny the fact, that here in India, especially in a Patcherie, where children see and hear so many things, and learn all that is bad, it is very difficult for parents to bring them up in the fear and love of God. Now this is just the reason why both father and mother should do all in their power in order that the children may get a good, religious education. By doing this, they will secure for themselves the greatest blessings for time and for eternity.

All the happiness of parents with regard to their children, is that they have *good children*, that is to say, children who treat them with every respect, and who obey all their orders cheerfully and without a murmur, not only indeed to show the love and reverence they have for their parents, and the pleasure they have in carrying out even their smallest commands, but also with a view of pleasing God after the example of Jesus Christ, who was subject and obedient to Joseph and Mary at Nazareth during his childhood. Such are the duties of children towards their parents, and the latter may be called happy indeed when Almighty God has blessed them with children who respect, obey, and love them. Such love and obedience are the greatest blessing to parents, as the Scripture says: "A virtuous child is the consolation, joy, satisfaction, and crown of his father." Prov. XVII. 6.

But how will parents be able to obtain this blessing? Answer, by bringing up their children in the fear and love of God. The reason is because he who loves God will also be anxious to love the Commandments of God, and a child who is instructed in the fear and love of God will keep particularly the great commandment God has given to all children: "Honour thy father and thy mother." Yes; it is a fact that children, who are imbued with religious principles, and have learned to fear and love the Lord are in every other respect good children, and the joy of their parents. When you see a child who does not behave well, showing little respect to his parents and causing great grief to them by disobedience and disrespect, then you may know at once that this child is neither pious nor good, and neglects his duties towards God. But, when you see boys or girls, who never omit their prayers, and often receive the Holy Sacraments, then you may conclude, for certain, that they likewise fulfil their duties towards their parents at home, and show them that reverence, obedience and love, which are the distinguishing marks of good children.

It lies in the power of every parent to have good children, and by giving them a good education to secure for themselves the greatest happiness on earth. Only fill their minds with religious principles, with a hatred of sin and a love of virtue; send them, if your means allow it, to a good school, where they are taught not only what they require in a worldly point of view, but also the great truths of our holy religion; see that they learn and understand their Catechism, and frequently encourage them to improve in this knowledge; watch over their conduct at home and abroad; do not allow them to join bad companions, nor to read such books as may tend to undermine their faith and be injurious to good morals; admonish and correct them, chastise them when they deserve it; but above all, give them by your conduct, the example of a truly Christian life.

The most that children learn, they learn from their parents, because their ordinary conversation is with them and because, as they love them the best, so they observe them the most. Children copy the very air, mien, habits, and manners of their parents. It is, therefore, of great consequence that parents should let their children see nothing in them, or hear anything from them, but what deserves imitation.

Now many parents are doing just the contrary, and it seems like a miracle that in spite of an entirely neglected education, there are still good, pious and innocent children in the Patcheries.

When a child is four or five years old, it should certainly know how to bless itself; it should be able to say the Lord's Prayer and Hail Mary, but in many cases the parents do not teach their children anything, and leave it all to the Priest visiting the school.

At seven years of age children are supposed to have come to years of discretion, and to be able to distinguish between right and wrong, between good and evil, consequently they can be guilty of mortal sins. They should be prepared for their first confession. But their parents take no interest in that, and are perhaps throwing obstacles in the way of the Priest, who insists upon the first Confession being made. But what about the children's first Communion? Alas! we see boys and girls of nearly fourteen years of age who have not as yet been to Communion, simply because their parents did not in the least encourage them. Thus it happens that such children go into service or are enlisted in the army, where they are quite out of the control of the Priest and of their parents, remaining ignorant of all that concerns the knowledge and practice of their religion.

It is also of the greatest importance that father and mother should watch the conduct of their children and not allow them to go to all sorts of places, nor join bad companions. Boys should be prohibited from staying in the barrack rooms where they pick up filthy and blasphemous language; girls should not be sent in the dark to the bazaar or canteen, where they are often seen standing about at shops and other places, chatting and laughing with dangerous persons. For real faults they should be punished by their parents. "The rod and reproof give wisdom, but the child that is left to his own will bringeth his mother shame" (Prov. XXIX. 15), and "He that spareth the rod hateth his son" (Prov. XIII. 24). Parents who neglect to correct their children become, in fact, accomplices of their children's sins. Let them remember what God said to Heli, the High Priest: "I will judge his house for ever, for iniquity; because he knew that his sons did wickedly, and did not chastise them." (I Kings, III. 13.) Many parents make a great mistake, when they punish a child for a trifling thing and merely out of anger, in a passion, while they overlook greater faults. For having broken a cup or glass they will chastise their son or daughter severely, but when they make use of bad language, and neglect their religious duties, nothing is said to them about it.

St. Jerome, a Doctor and Father of the Church, was once requested by a Roman lady to advise her concerning the education of her daughter. He replied in a few words: "Take care she sees nothing in you or in her father, which, if she imitates, she may offend God." Would to heaven, Christian parents, that none of your children saw anything in you, which, if they imitate, they may offend God!

Let not your children see you in a violent passion, that breaks out into cursing and swearing; for if they imitate you in this they will offend God.

Let them never hear a lie or immodest word from your lips; for if they imitate you in this they will offend God.

Let them never see in you any carelessness in the service of God, neglect of prayer, and of the Holy Sacraments; for if they imitate you in this they will offend God.

It is true that in certain cases parents gain very little in spite of all their exertions to give their children a good education; but these are exceptions. With good reason we may ask what would have become of this or that boy or girl, if he or she had not received a good education? Or rather, what has become of so many children whose education was neglected? Many men would not be in misery if they had had parents who took good care of them whilst young, but unfortunately they were neglected and had to shift for themselves. How many parents can tell a sad tale in this respect! You need not go very far to find a mother complaining of her adult children, and now she is heart-broken on account of the treatment she receives at the hands of those who should be the joy, consolation, and support of her old age. They must confess that such are the results of a neglected education; they must strike their breast and say: "It is my own fault, my most grievous fault! Ah, if I had given these children a religious education; if I had sent them to a good Catholic school; if I had shown them the way to the house of God; if I had not overlooked their faults but punished them instead of allowing them to do what they liked; if I had but given them a good example!" Alas! it is too true; "**What a man sows, the same** he will reap." I have sown bad seed, and now I have the fruit. Jesus Christ asks: "Do men gather grapes from thorns, or figs from thistles?" Behold, your children degenerated into thorns and thistles. What fruit can you expect? But such is the just judgment which Almighty God inflicts upon parents even in this world. They have not taught their children the fear and love of God, and therefore these children have not learned to respect and love their parents.

But what should above all induce parents to discharge their duties, in the best possible manner, towards their children, is the thought that their own salvation depends on it. "If thou wilt enter into life keep the Commandments," says our Lord. Wherefore parents cannot be saved, when they neglect their children's education. Although they may be pious, fervent in their prayers, charitable to the poor, and good Christians in every other respect, yet if they be guilty of neglecting their children they cannot be saved.

Besides this Almighty God threatens with woe, that is to say with eternal damnation all those who scandalise the little ones. "Woe to him by whom scandal comes, it were better for him that a mill-stone should be hanged about his neck, and that he should be drowned in the depth of the sea." This curse has a greater weight when they are your own little ones, when you have neglected and scandalised those whom

God the Father entrusted to your care; whom God the Son has redeemed at the price of His blood; whom God the Holy Ghost has made His temples by the Sacrament of Baptism.

You must not forget that you take the place of God, and that these children are *His* property more than *yours*. You are their parents according to the flesh, but you did not give them their immortal souls. God will ask those souls from you on the day of judgment—and what a cause of grief it will be to you, should you see them on the left side of the Judge among the damned, and that, through your unpardonable fault in neglecting to train them in youth in the knowledge and love of Almighty God!

CONCLUSION.

At this stage your friendly guide bids you good-bye for the present; not because he has nothing more to say, but because the book would transgress the limits fixed for it.

However do not be satisfied with having perused this book once only, as you would do with a novel or a periodical. These instructions must be read over and over again, and you must regulate your life accordingly.

Those who have been at Aldershot will still remember the regularity of Camp life. The only public clock (at least some years ago) is the great Sebastapol Bell, on which the hours are chimed. After a certain hour at night the passenger is challenged with, "Who goes there?" and when the reply is made, "A friend!" The sentinel resumes his beat with the response: "Pass, friend, all is well." Now, in referring to the sentry's challenge, think what a solemn time it will be, when you shall be saluted as above, and how you ought to be a good Christian Soldier, so that when you are, at the closing scene of your life, challenged by the words:" Who comes there? the Master's reply will be: "Pass friend, all is well."

A. M. D. G.

www.ingramcontent.com/pod-product-compliance
Lightning Source LLC
Chambersburg PA
CBHW032000230426
43672CB00010B/2217